D1556620

ACONCAGUA
AND THE SOUTHERN ANDES

*I grew up in this city, my poetry was born between
the mountain and the river, it took its voice from the rain,
and like the timber, it steeped itself in the forests.*
Pablo Neruda (Chilean poet)

About the author

Jim Ryan is a civil engineer by profession. A seasoned traveller his life-long passion for the mountains has taken him to many remote places. He has travelled, and written extensively, on some of the great walks of the world, such as in Nepal, Lesotho in South Africa, Kilimanjaro and the island of Reunion in the Indian Ocean. His guide to *Carrauntoohil and The MacGillycuddy Reeks* in Ireland continues to be a best seller.

Jim has a special interest in geology. The mountain of Aconcagua and its region made a significant impression on him on his first journey there as part of an expedition in 1999/2000. He noted the lack of information on one of the world's great mountains and produced this guidebook.

Acknowledgements

Thanks are due to Sue Ryan for her patience and proof reading, to Fergus Humphries for producing the maps, to Lois Sparling of Cicerone for her patience, to Eduardo Depetris, Pablo Reguera, Sebastian Tetilla, Angel Tetilla, Marco Garrido Dasté, Pedro Marzolo, Nito Giordano, Pancho Medina, Elias Lira, Gisela Palacios and to Professor John Gamble of University College Cork for identifying samples of rock.

CONTENTS

INDEX OF MAPS AND ILLUSTRATIONS

Advice to Readers

Readers are advised that, while every effort is made by our authors to ensure the accuracy of our guidebooks as they go to print, changes can occur during the lifetime of a particular edition. Please check the Cicerone website (**www.cicerone.co.uk**) for any updates before planning your trip. It is also advisable to check information on such things as transport, accommodation and shops locally. Even rights of way can be altered over time. We are always grateful for information about any discrepancies between a guidebook and the facts on the ground, sent by email to info@cicerone.co.uk or by post to Cicerone, 2 Police Square, Milnthorpe LA7 7PY, United Kingdom.

Map Key

~~	ridges
≈≈≈	roads
– – – – –	route
··············	Vacas valley route
··············	normal route
═══════	fresh water pipe
	national boundary
= = = =	tunnel
++++++++++	railway
(glacier symbol)	glacier
⌒⌒	river
(lagoon symbol)	water/lagoon
■	building
)(	bridge
●	town
▲	summit
Λ	camp
†	statue
⊕	airport

Contours

	6500–7000m
	6000–6500m
	5500–6000m
	5000–5500m
	4500–5000m
	4000–4500m
	3500–4000m
	3000–3500m
	2500–3000m

ACONCAGUA
AND THE SOUTHERN ANDES

by
Jim Ryan

2 POLICE SQUARE, MILNTHORPE, CUMBRIA LA7 7PY
www.cicerone.co.uk

© Jim Ryan 2004, 2009
Second edition 2009
ISBN: 978 1 85284 587 2
First edition 2004
ISBN-10: 1 85284 455 8
ISBN-13: 978 1 85284 455 4

Printed by MCC Graphics, Spain
A catalogue record for this book is available from the British Library.
All photographs are by the author unless otherwise stated.

Warning

Mountaineering can be a dangerous activity carrying a risk of personal injury or death. It should be undertaken only by those with a full understanding of the risks and with the training and experience to evaluate them. Mountaineers should be appropriately equipped for the routes undertaken. Every care and effort has been taken in the preparation of this book but the user should be aware that conditions can be highly variable and can change quickly. Holds may become loose or fall off, rockfall can affect the character of a route and, in winter, snow and avalanche conditions must be carefully considered. These can materially affect the seriousness of a climb, tour or expedition.

The mountains described in this book reach high altitudes. There are health risks in high-altitude climbing, such as pulmonary and cerebral oedema (that can cause sickness and death); extreme temperatures (that can cause frostbite); and traversing over ice (the risk of falling or sliding). Climbers are advised to be in good physical condition; to acclimatise, and not to ascend too quickly; to keep a constant check on saturated oxygen level; to descend if they feel unwell; to consult a doctor before attempting high-altitude climbs; and to bring adequate medication, gear and clothing with them. Training on ice climbing, ropework and high-altitude problems is essential for the uninitiated.

Therefore, except for any liability which cannot be excluded by law, neither Cicerone nor the author can accept liability for damage of any nature (including damage to property, personal injury or death) arising directly or indirectly from the information in this book.

Front cover: A mule train returns along the Relinchos Valley

PERU

BRAZIL

BOLIVIA

CHILE

PARAGUAY

▲ Aconcagua
● Mendoza

Santiago ●

ARGENTINA   URUGUAY

● Buenos
Aries

Map of
South America

N

Falklands
🏝 (Malvinas)

Tierra del Fuego

9

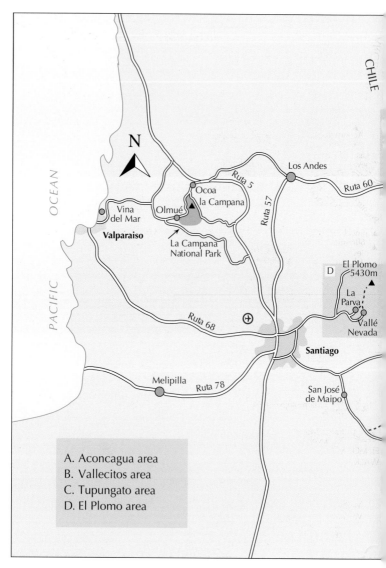

CHILE

N

OCEAN

PACIFIC

Los Andes

Ruta 5

Ruta 60

Ocoa
la Campana

Ruta 57

Olmué

Vina
del Mar

Valparaiso

La Campana
National Park

El Plomo
5430m

D

La
Parva

Ruta 68

Vallé
Nevada

Santiago

Melipilla

Ruta 78

San José
de Maipo

A. Aconcagua area
B. Vallecitos area
C. Tupungato area
D. El Plomo area

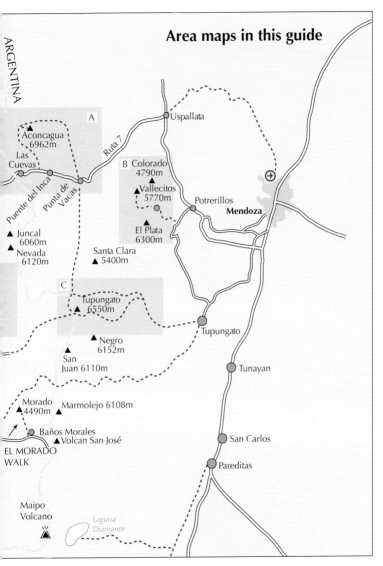

Area maps in this guide

ARGENTINA

A

▲ Aconcagua
6962m

Las
Cuevas

Ruta 7

Uspallata

B ▲ Colorado
4790m

Puente del Inca

Punta de Vacas

▲ Vallecitos
5770m

Potrerillos

Mendoza

▲ Juncal
6060m

▲ El Plata
6300m

▲ Nevada
6120m

Santa Clara
▲ 5400m

C

▲ Tupungato
6550m

Tupungato

▲ Negro
6152m

Tunayan

▲
San
Juan 6110m

Morado
▲4490m Marmolejo 6108m ▲

● Baños Morales
▲Volcan San José

San Carlos

EL MORADO
WALK

Pareditas

Maipo
Volcano

🌋

Laguna
Diamante

A well-worn path through penitentes out of Plaza de Mulas

FOREWORD

Aconcagua is not merely a mountain to me. It is my life. As a mountain guide I have summitted Aconcagua too many times to recall.

Over three decades I have witnessed the number of climbers grow every year. In those three decades there has been more than a twelve-fold increase in numbers, and the increase continues.

We who serve these climbers must adapt to cater for the numbers. A guidebook such as this helps in this regard, and it improves our services to those who climb our mountain.

The degree of written material on Aconcagua when Jim's first edition was published was sparse. His map was one of the first detailed maps of the area in print. His focus was to produce a practical guide for the ordinary trekker, and he has succeeded.

It is up to us all to keep the mountain clean. Sadly cleanliness was neglected in the past, but the **Leave no Trace** policies are beginning to show results.

I welcome the new edition of Jim's book with its various updates and additions. I know it will sell as well as the first edition.

Sebastian Tetilla
Mendoza

The glacier above Plaza Argentina with penitentes in the foreground

PREFACE

This book is intended primarily for the many thousands of people who travel each year to climb the highest peak of the Americas – Aconcagua, travelling into either Santiago or Mendoza and remaining in the region before returning. For these people, this is a comprehensive guide. You won't need to carry any other books.

For every eight who attempt the peak only two succeed, the majority failing because of altitude sickness or the weather, but also lack of preparation. A considerable section of the book is devoted to advice on acclimatisation and good preparations. For those who prefer to acclimatise on nearby mountains, choices are offered near Mendoza (Vallecitos 5770m) and near Santiago (El Plomo 5430m). Many will want to get to the Aconcagua Provincial Park and acclimatise there and treks are detailed near and within the park with this in mind. A special wilderness trek within Tupungato Provincial Park to the site of a plane that crashed into a mountain to be swallowed in its glacier and re-emerge fifty years later is also described.

The central regions of Chile and Argentina have much to offer besides the Andes and these attractions are described here for trekkers forced to abandon the climb because of altitude sickness or the weather, or with time to spare. Information is also included on the geology, flora and fauna, customs and traditions of the region, and even the language itself, to help you get the most from your visit. Santiago and Mendoza have had a special relationship since their foundations and the history of their peoples, customs and architecture is fascinating. Finally, practical information is included in the appendices about places to stay and eat, shop and hire gear.

Changes since the first edition

Over the past four years there have been significant changes in the Southern Andes: the Mendocino government has introduced many new regulations, particularly relating to waste and protection of the environment; there are new restrictions on routes and new impositions for minors; the permit office has moved; an excellent new topographical map of the region has been published; evacuation by helicopter from Plaza de Mulas and Plaza Argentina, ordered by the park doctor, is now free of charge; the Confluencia campsite has moved (again); global warming has curtailed the glaciers and reduced the degree of penitentes; and high inflation has caused costs in Argentina to escalate.

The new edition of this guidebook reflects these changes on the ground. Also, a day trip to the Maipo volcano has been added to the many things to see and do around Mendoza and the climb of Tupungato from Chile has been expanded.

Jim Ryan

Trekkers returning along the Vacas Valley route below Plaza Argentina

INTRODUCTION

The mountain of Aconcagua in the southern Andes is the highest peak in the world outside the Himalayas. It is the highest of the seven continental summits after Everest and it offers the climber the best value in terms of altitude gained for effort expended.

The purist might contend that climbing in double plastic boots, with crampons and an ice axe, in temperatures of -20°C, can hardly be classified as a 'trek'. Nevertheless, Aconcagua does require very little technical expertise and it provides valuable high altitude experience for non-climbers.

In recent years the pursuit of climbing and hill walking has attracted more and more enthusiasts. Travel to far off places has become more popular and easier to arrange. Mountain guides clog the internet with advertisements for their adventure holidays. For those who tire of the commonplace, goals such as Kilimanjaro, Island Peak and Aconcagua are there to provide the adventure.

Aconcagua is seen as an essential stepping-stone for those with eyes on the big prize – Everest. However, the serious alpinist will have to rub shoulders with the adventurous trekker. As

Suspension Bridge over Horcones River on the Normal Route

for any mountain, there are numerous routes up Aconcagua. The majority are categorised as extremely difficult, but two routes are available that require minimal technical expertise and they are the routes described in detail here.

The area of South America in which Aconcagua is situated is quite civilised, transport is good, and there is an established infrastructure for mountain access. There are no nasties in the region, such as snakes, mosquitoes or wild cats. The people are friendly, food is great and language is not a particular barrier. The region has many other attractions, such as the vineyards of Chile and Mendoza, white water rafting, the beach at Viña del Mar, rodeos and numerous other scenic and cultural items of interest.

Lest the impression be conveyed that Aconcagua is a bed of roses the following caution is appropriate. The mountain is bleak and harsh. The winds on Aconcagua can be unrelenting and the temperatures severe.

The incidence of failure as a result of altitude sickness and weather is particularly high. Many climbers arrive unprepared for the cold and the altitude and have to make return visits for second attempts.

There are no less than 164 peaks in the Himalayas that have greater altitudes than Aconcagua. In the Americas, however, Aconcagua tops a list of 43 peaks, all in South America, ahead of Denali (Mount McKinley) in North America.

Alpinists consider Aconcagua to be much more difficult than a large proportion of its Himalayan cousins. This they attribute to its harsh environment, its unpredictable weather, the dreaded Canaleta scree slope that must be overcome at 6800m and its long distance to basecamp. The relative distance of Aconcagua from the equator, compared to the Himalayas, is considered to be a factor in terms of weather and altitude. The further one travels from the equator the thinner is the earth's atmosphere.

THE CONTINENTIAL HIGH POINTS

	Mountain	Height
Asia	Everest	8850m
South America	**Aconcagua**	**6962m**
North America	Denali	6194m
Africa	Kilimanjaro	5963m
Europe	Elbrus	5633m
Antarctica	Vinson Massif	4897m
Oceania	Puncak Jaya	4884m

THE 12 HIGHEST PEAKS OF THE AMERICAS

	Height	Country
Aconcagua	**6962m**	**Argentina**
Ojos del Salado	6880m	Argentina-Chile
Pissis	6779m	Argentina
Mercedario	6770m	Argentina
Huascarán	6768m	Peru
Bonete Chico	6759m	Argentina
Llullaillaco	6723m	Argentina-Chile
Yerupajá	6634m	Peru
Tres Cruces	6620m	Argentina-Chile
Coropuna	6613m	Peru
Incahuasi	6601m	Argentina-Chile
Tupungato	6550m	Argentina-Chile

TWO TREKKING ROUTES

Every mountain has a diversity of routes to the summit, and Aconcagua is no exception. This guide covers the two most popular, non-technical ascents, with a brief reference to the route around to the north via Plaza Guanaco and the more advanced direct route up the Polish Glacier.

Over 70 per cent of all climbers take the **Normal Route.** This is also known as the Horcones Valley Route. The approach is from the south, 36km over a rough river valley to basecamp at Plaza de Mulas. From Plaza de Mulas the route swings around to the east, over steep ground, eventually turning directly south to the summit.

The second popular trekking route is known as the **Vacas Valley Route**, but is also known as the Polish Glacier Route, or even the False Polish Glacier Route. It is 47km from the road head to basecamp at Plaza Argentina. Initially the direction is, like the Normal Route, due north for 31km, then making a left turn to the west and going a further 16km up the Relinchos River valley.

Both routes join high up the mountain, below a small ruined hut, called Independencia, at 6250m.

Via the Normal Route the summit will be visible for much of the journey to basecamp, whereas on the Vacas Valley Route it only comes into view when you reach the left hand turn after 31km. The average time (subject to acclimatisation) to the summit and back to the road head is 12 days via the Normal Route and 14 days on the Vacas Valley Route.

At basecamp, Plaza de Mulas, on the Normal Route, there is a hotel, fairly basic in comforts, but it does have a telephone. There are no such luxuries at Plaza Argentina.

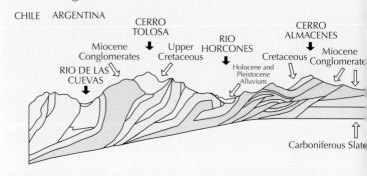

Geological Cross Section

CHILE   ARGENTINA

CERRO
TOLOSA

CERRO
ALMACENES

RIO
HORCONES

Miocene
Conglomerates

Upper
Cretaceous

Cretaceous

Miocene
Conglomerate

RIO DE LAS
CUEVAS

Holocene and
Pleistocene
Alluvium

Carboniferous Slate

Nevertheless, the Vacas Valley route is less crowded and more picturesque. Consequently there is more bird life and even the possibility of seeing some wild guanacos.

The Vacas Valley Route is tougher and longer than the Normal Route. However, for those not acclimatised, this pays dividends leaving them better prepared for summit day. Acclimatisation on another mountain, such as at Vallecitos or El Plomo, then climbing via the Normal Route, is an ideal option.

LOCATION

Aconcagua is located entirely within the Republic of Argentina, very close to the border with Chile. Halfway south to the middle of Chile and below the Tropic of Capricorn, it is

20

in the province of Mendoza and the department of Las Heras.

The Aconcagua Provincial Park lies immediately off the main road that links the cities of Mendoza in Argentina and Santiago in Chile. Of the 13 passes over the Andes between the two countries this is the only paved road. On the southern side of the road another of Mendoza's provincial parks – The Tupungato Provincial Park – begins.

The nearest village on the main road is Puente del Inca, which is 15km inside the Argentina/Chile border, 186km from Mendoza and 169km from Santiago. Between the starting points of the two trekking routes lies the village of Los Penitentes, a ski resort with a cable car up to the mountains (closed during the summer).

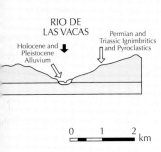

RIO DE
LAS VACAS

Permian and
Triassic Ignimbritics
and Pyroclastics

Holocene and
Pleistocene
Alluvium

0   1   2 km

GEOLOGY

Charles Darwin was the first explorer to examine the geology of the high Andes. His 1835 sketch of the Puente del Inca rock formation remains a classic. The German geologist, Walter Schiller, however, is recognised as the father of Andean geology, perhaps only surpassed in recent times by Victor Ramos.

The geological deposits of Aconcagua fall into three periods
• the base sedimentary rocks
• the higher volcanic rocks, and
• the glacial and alluvial deposits.

The base sedimentary rocks range in age from the Carboniferous, through the Permian, Triassic and Jurassic into the Cretaceous period. So they are approximately 100 to 300 million years old. The base rocks under the Vacas Valley are the oldest rocks. These Carboniferous slates

can be seen on the high ground east of Puente del Inca, and above Los Penitentes.

The Permian ignimbritic and pyroclastic rocks that form the sides of the Vacas Valley are the second oldest. Up at the south face of Aconcagua, near Plaza Francia, red Jurassic and early Cretaceous limestones are visible at the western base. On the walk in to Confluencia you pass a grey limestone boulder field. These boulders have come down from a Jurassic formation high on the mountain.

Tectonic plate movements have lifted up and twisted these rocks. Fault lines and dramatic folds are common. Volcanic activity accompanied the tectonic plate movements, so that these older deposits support extensive masses of volcanic lavas and ashes of more recent date. The convergence of the oceanic plate and the South American plate, estimated to be happening at a rate of 90 to 100 millimetres per annum, has resulted in a number of major earthquakes in the region, notably one in 1861 which destroyed Mendoza and another as recent as 1985 with an epicentre in Valparaiso.

Metamorphic heat has transformed some of the sedimentary rocks. Great mountains of trachyte rise from the sedimentary base. In his 1884 treatise *Der Vulcan Aconcagua* the German naturalist and climber, Paul Gussfeldt, postulated that there was probably once a crater on the south summit.

The predominant rock found on Aconcagua is a grey rock with black

21

particles. It is not unlike sandstone, but has been positively identified as a volcanic Andesite. This same rock outcrops on the summit and can be seen on many of the scree slopes. Above the Berlin camp, below Rocas Blancas, on the west and north sides, there are areas of thermal clay. These are yellowish in colour and contain sulphur. This suggests that Aconcagua is an extinct volcano or an uplifted volcano, perched on top of a sedimentary base.

The river valleys south of the mountain contain deep deposits of gravel from four periods of glaciation and from natural erosion. Ice and frost on the mountain account for much of this erosion. In the Horcones valley these glacial and alluvial deposits are up to five metres deep, cut through by the river. The Horcones and Vacas rivers have a high discharge and flow very fast in the summer season, as the snow and ice above melts. The water

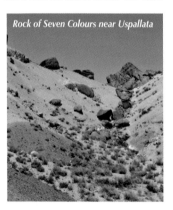

Rock of Seven Colours near Uspallata

is dark red in colour, as it conveys its load of suspended solids down to deposit it in the valleys below.

TOPOGRAPHY

The central Andes is divided into four north-south *cordilleras*. Immediately west of Mendoza is the relatively low **Precordillera**. This is the mountain range that blocks a view of the high peaks from the city. Beyond it to the west is the **Frontal Cordillera** that includes peaks such as Vallecitos (5770m) and El Plata (6300m). The **Principal Cordillera** includes Aconcagua (6962m), Tupungato (6550m) and El Plomo (5430m). Finally, west of Santiago, is the **Coastal Cordillera** that has mountains such as La Campana (1880m) and Roble Alto (2198m).

From the Vallecitos area there is a mountain range that stretches across in a northeast-southwest direction from the Frontal Cordillera towards Tupungato in the Principal Cordillera. This range is known as Cordón del Plata. It includes El Plata (6300m) and Vallecitos (5770m).

The climbing history of Aconcagua documents many attempts at finding a route to the summit, via the various valleys, over glaciers and so on – a good indication of how difficult the terrain is. There are no fewer than 13 peaks with an altitude over 5000m that encircle Aconcagua.

The jagged appearances of the mountains at high-level contrast with the smooth river valleys below. Sharp

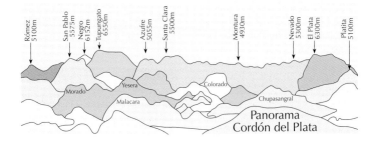

Rómez 5100m | San Pablo 5575m | Negro 6152m | Tupungato 6550m | Azufre 5055m | Santa Clara 5500m | Montura 4930m | Nevado 5300m | El Plata 6300m | Platita 5100m

Morado | Yesera | Colorado | Chupasangral

Malacara

**Panorama
Cordón del Plata**

mountain features mellow into scree slopes that sweep down to the rivers. Landslides are common.

There are five main glaciers in the Aconcagua area. The most significant is the Polish Glacier which covers the eastern side of the mountain. Next in importance is the Horcones Inferior Glacier, which swings around from behind the Mirador mountain (directly south of Aconcagua) to run down to within a few kilometres of the Confluencia campsite. Hardly recognisable from the air because it is covered in scree, it is 20 metres deep in places. A slowly moving mass of ice, it groans and squeaks as it slides down the valley.

Minor glaciers abound. Some, like the Horcones Inferior Glacier, are covered in rocks and scree, tens of metres thick, slowly moving down the valleys. Others are white and covered with *penitentes*.

The penitentes of Aconcagua are a feature of the region (and are the origin of more than one place name in this guide). These ice spikes can be as low as a few centimetres or as high as four metres. Caused by the very cold winds on the mountain, the penitentes are set out in a linear pattern, usually with about half a metre between spikes. Wonderful to photograph, particularly when white, they present a formidable barrier to the climber.

The Horcones Valley approach has an area near the road head that provides a 'picture postcard' view of the mountain. With the harsh white outline of the peak in the background Laguna Horcones is a green, lush picnic point three kilometres from the road.

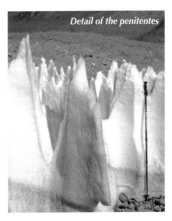

Detail of the penitentes

23

Sightseers will often drive in off the main highway, away from the noise of the busy traffic, to the tranquillity of the water's edge.

WILDLIFE

During the summer low growing cactus and other wild flowers provide minimal ground cover in as far as Confluencia on the Horcones Valley route and as far as Plaza Argentina on the Vacas Valley route. There are small areas of grass, more frequent in the Vacas Valley, and you may even see cows grazing on this grass in the Vacas Valley (*Valley of Cows*).

Orchids and calandrinia are plentiful in the spring and early summer. In November the viola is just beginning to show flower at its rims.

There is a distinct probability that, on a trek to the summit, you will not see a single live animal, not even a rodent, but you will see an abundance of small birds, particularly on the Vacas Valley route. Larger birds are rare and there are few of any size above the basecamps. Small lizards

Calandrinia

Violas emerge in early Spring and prepare to bloom

will often be seen, scurrying in the rocks in the Vacas Valley below Pampa de Leñas.

The South American condor is a very large bird that hovers in the sky. Another bird of prey, the *carancho andino*, has the same features as the condor, but with a degree of white on the wings and rear body. They also hover and are often mistaken for condors but are much smaller. A condor has a wingspan of over three metres, and the ends of its wings have a band of silver feathers and are distinctly serrated. In between the condor and the carancho in size is the *jote cabeza negra* (or, if it has a red head, *jote cabeza roja*). This is also a black vulture that hovers, but it has no white feathers.

The small birds that hop around the lower campsites are known as *testes* or *cometinos de gay*. They are Sierra finches and have dark heads and yellow breasts. Scraps of food will entice them into photo range.

A bird that you will hear but seldom see is the *perdicita*. It is the same size as a thrush and has the same mottled wings, but its head is grey and its legs orange. The perdicita's call sounds like a squeaky pump that needs oil.

On the El Plomo trek there will be many birds at Piedra Numerada, including the noisy perdicita. The brown birds with grey breasts and a golden scalp are *dormilonas fraile*.

The red fox, hares and guanacos are the only animals you might see, and the guanaco only in the Vacas Valley. The red fox of the Andes, *Dusicyon culpaeus,* is the same size as a domestic dog. Its red fur is generally grey-white on its back. The fox will seldom be seen during the daytime, but may wander around the lower campsites at night, searching for scraps. Beware: it can carry rabies.

Guanacos, *Llama guanicoe,* are relatives of the common South American domesticated llama. They have a curled yellow fur with a white belly. Roaming in small herds, they are very nervous animals that avoid

A guanaco

human presence. Guanacos are amazingly agile. Upon detecting potential predators they will run high into the hills. The herd will generally consist of several females and their young and one dominant male. They make high-pitched calls, and their droppings are similar to those of sheep.

Ancient History

The ancient history of southern Chile and Argentina is not well documented. Human beings are thought to have crossed from North to South America approximately 15,000 years ago, reaching down as far as Tierra del Fuego some 10,000 years later. Tribes such as the Araucanos, Aymaras and later the Wari are believed to have been early inhabitants of Chile before the Incas. The Mapuche people lived south of Santiago and dominated most of Argentina.

The Incas, Mapuche and Huarpes

At some point between the later part of the 15th century and the middle of the 16th century the Incas took control of northern Chile, but were repelled from Argentina by the Mapuche in the south and the Huarpes in the Mendoza area. There is evidence that they held the mountains in high regard, that they climbed them and used the mountains to offer sacrifices to their gods. A guanaco discovered in 1947 between the north and south

Representation of the Aconcagua mummy at the Museo Cornelio Moyano, Mendoza

ridge of Aconcagua was considered to have been brought there as a sacrifice and the ridge has since been known as Cresta del Guanaco.

Mummies have also been uncovered on this and other peaks. On the nearby peak of Cerro Piramidal, for instance, the mummified remains of a young girl were discovered. Another was unearthed on top of the 6723m mountain of Llullaillaco. On the summit of El Plomo, at 5430m, overlooking the city of Santiago, there is an Inca altar and a burial site where the mummified remains of a child were discovered in 1954.

In Mendoza's Parque General San Martin there is a small natural history museum, *Museo Cornelio Moyano*. Housed in the museum until relatively recently (now in the Criant nearby) were the remains of the mummy found at 5300m on the southwestern side of Aconcagua.

Advent of the Spanish Conquistadors
The Spanish conquests of the Incas by Pisarro in the middle of the 16th century were to change the history of the entire western side of South America. In 1520 Magellan had discovered the straits that allowed trade between Spain and Asia. Spanish expeditions from the north eventually led to the invasion by Valdivia, the great Spanish general, who founded the city of Santiago.

The first contact between the Spanish and the Huarpas was in 1551, when an exploratory expedition was sent over the Andes. Ten years later, in 1561 the then captain general of Santiago, General Mendoza, sent his captain, Pedro de Castillo, with a major force over the Andes and there the city of Mendoza was founded, and called after him. Thus Mendoza became a province of Santiago, despite the enormous obstacle of the Andes in between. Cultural and commercial ties between the two cities that developed in the 16th century remain today.

Decades of conflict followed with the Mapuche. General Valdivia himself was killed by them in 1553. Then, in 1641, a treaty was reached leaving the Mapuche autonomous below the River Biobio. Only as late as the 19th century did the Mapuche integrate to become part of Chile.

Spanish colonial rule followed in both countries until the early part of the 19th century, when Napoleon invaded Spain. The consequent uncertainty ended with Chile declaring independence in 1810, and Argentina following in 1816. It was not until 1818, however, that the great heroes of Chile, José de San Martin and Bernardo O'Higgins formally created the new nation, following the final defeat of the Royalists.

Mendoza suffered a severe earthquake in 1861. With the epicentre being at the heart of the city the devastation was enormous, and thousands were killed. Relief for the homeless came from around the globe and helped to have the city rebuilt.

An earthquake on the Chilean side accounted for 20,000 deaths in 1906. Measured at 8.6 on the Richter scale it had its epicentre in Valparaiso.

Recent History

Both countries have had colourful recent pasts. Chile's wealth was initially built on copper, silver and nitrates. Argentina's economy was largely centred on cattle and sheep. Nowadays wine production is a relatively new source of wealth for both countries, Chile producing more than Argentina. It is interesting to note that *Aconcagua* is one of the five demarcated wine regions of Chile. Chile produces and exports fruit, and among its natural resources copper is significant.

The production of maize, soya and other crops continues to be significant for Argentina, and Argentinean beef has an international reputation. Garlic is an important Mendocino product. South of Mendoza there are a number of small oil wells.

Water from the Andes provides irrigation for vineyards and cultivation

Tupungato in the background over the Norton vineyard

Santiago's modern architecture

on both sides of the mountains. It provides drinking water, and the dam at Porterillos provides electricity. Similarly a dam on the Rio Colorado provides electricity on the Chilean side.

Chile courted socialism, in 1886 with president Balmaceda, in 1920 with president Palma, and finally in 1970 with Salvador Allende. A workers-supported military coup brought Juan Peron to power in Argentina in 1946. Military rule continued until President Galtieri took on the British in his ill-fated invasion of the Falklands in 1982.

In 1985 Mendoza was rocked by another earthquake, but the damage to the relatively new low-rise buildings was not significant. Valparaiso was the epicentre of Chile's most recent earthquakes in 1971 and 1985.

Chile has a population of just less than 15 million, of which the

Mapuche account for nearly one million. The majority of the population is *mestizo*, which is a mix of Hispanic and Indian. By contrast the vast majority of Argentina's 36 million people are of European decent. Italy was the origin of many original Mendocinos. Their attachment to their Italian ancestors is marked by a major festival in March every year, centred around Plaza Italia.

The people who live and work in the mountain region, on either side of the border, have distinctive Indo-European features.

Chile suffered under the regime that followed Allende and many fled the country. Over the past decade there has been a gradual return of these exiles, many from Spain. The returning exiles have brought back with them new ideas that has sparked a revitalisation of the culture of Chile. This is most clearly seen in its modern architecture. In Valparaiso there is a school of architecture that has achieved world standing.

Of Chile's current domestic problems the claim by the Mapuche for their land rights has never gone away. The Mapuche contend that many millions of hectares of traditional Mapuche lands were taken by the government and sold. A similar, but not as contentious, problem with the Mapuches exists over the border in Argentina where Mapuche demonstrators are squatting at the United Colours of Benneton sheep farm.

In the countryside around Mendoza and Tupungato there are many Bolivian migrant workers who toil in the sun cultivating vegetables. The Mendocinos tend to look down on them.

The United Nations' Index of 2007/8 on poverty ranked Argentina in 38th place and Chile in 40th place, both higher than any other South American country. The centres of cities such as Buenos Aires and Santiago are clearly affluent but there is deep poverty in the countryside, particularly in Chile.

The collapse of the Argentinean economy in 2001/2 was a turning point for this once-great nation. Inflation during that year reached 300 per cent, unemployment soared and political unrest was rife. Within a brief two years Argentinean society had tumbled from its perch as the most affluent in South America to one that resembled its poorer northern neighbours. The economy has since steadied, and confidence is gradually being restored. However, as both countries entered 2009, both now with female

heads of state, the Argentineans were hoping that the 2008 inflation rate of 26 per cent would fall, while the Chileans were working to bolster the economy against the looming world recession.

Argentinean–Chilean Relationships

Argentina and Chile have been close to war on a number of occasions, all related to border disputes. Queen Victoria arbitrated between them in 1902 and Queen Elizabeth in 1977. It was not until the 1990s that the presidents of both countries made a lasting peace.

The enormous statue on the border, Christ the Redeemer (Cristo Redentor), was erected by both countries as a sign of peace after the 1902 treaty. The area on which the statue was built, on the original old road, had been a particularly disputed one, so it was symbolically erected on the newly-agreed border. The inscription on its plaque reads 'These mountains will fall before the peace between our countries is broken'.

Although the border has been the main source of dispute there has always been a good relationship between the cities of Santiago and Mendoza. The proximity of Mendoza to Santiago, rather than to its national capital, Buenos Aires, and the excellent road and air connections, are undoubtedly factors in this relationship. The Spanish that is spoken in Mendoza is more akin to Chilean Spanish than to Argentinean Spanish.

A trip to the seaside, for Mendocinos, has always been via Santiago to Viña del Mar.

CLIMBING HISTORY

The mountain pass over the Andes to the south of Aconcagua, now Route 7 from Santiago to Mendoza, was an ancient Inca trail, and the mountain is clearly visible from the pass. This pass was used by José de San Martin and Bernardo O'Higgins to bring the 'Great Army of the Andes' down into Chile to defeat the Spanish in 1818.

Charles Darwin visited the region in 1835, and is reputed to have experienced earth tremors during his excursion ashore from the Beagle. Paul Gussfeldt, a German climber and naturalist, made an unsuccessful attempt at the summit in 1883.

In late 1896 the Englishman, Edward Fitzgerald, led a serious expedition. In his team were the Swiss climber Matthias Zurbriggen and another English climber Stuart Vines.

They set off from the mountain pass up the Vacas Valley, decided this was an impossible route, and returned to try the Lower Horcones Valley. Concluding that the south face was too difficult they returned to Confluencia and proceeded up the Normal Route.

After many weeks on the mountain Matthias Zurbriggen arrived on the summit on 14 January 1897. A month later Vines and an Italian porter named Nicola Lanti summitted.

The Polish Glacier on the eastern side of Aconcagua

Fitzgerald himself unfortunately never made it due to altitude sickness. He did, however, write a detailed account of his expedition, listing the conditions he encountered and the flora and fauna he had identified. This treatise remains today as an important document, not only in relation to Aconcagua, but also to the early studies of the Andes.

In March 1934 four Polish climbers, Konstanty Narkievitcz-Jodko, Stefan Osiecki, Wictor Ostowski and Stefan Dasyinski, ascended via the Polish Glacier. Part of a six-man party, they had ascended via the Vacas and Relinchos valleys. Severe weather had kept the party pinned on the glacier at 6300m, until they could make the decisive thrust to the summit. The Polish Glacier is named after them.

A French team travelled up the Lower Horcones Valley in 1954, and established a campsite (now known as Plaza Francia) under the south face. One month later six of the team reached the summit. It was late in the evening and they descended via the Normal Route. However, they were lucky to be picked up by other climbers, and they suffered severe frostbite.

The Argentinean army controlled the area until 1980, imposing many restrictions. In 1983 the area was declared a provincial park, opening the way to its popularity. Argentina has 22 national parks, yet, although Aconcagua attracts many thousands of visitors every year, it has not yet been elevated to national park status.

During the first open season in 1983 346 people climbed the mountain. In the 2002/3 season this had risen to almost six thousand (3800 climbers and 2132 low level trekkers), more than a ten-fold increase,

Trekkers in the Horcones Valley

and in 2007 the figure was 7500. The mountain inevitably suffered under this traffic.

As early as 1990 the government decided on a programme of cleaning and maintenance. Mules were taken as high as Independencia to remove rubbish. Strict procedures were adopted to keep the mountain clean, with refuse sacks being issued to all climbers. These restrictions on waste have recently been further reinforced. It is only permissible now to camp in the designated campsites, and climbers above the lower camps must contract with a service provider to accept and dispose of human faeces.

In 1992 the hotel was constructed near Plaza de Mulas. The worrying incidences of rock fall, particularly one that destroyed ten tents, forced the authorities to move Plaza des Mulas in 1997. Confluencia was also moved in 1999 to control pollution.

There are various recordings of ascents and descents over the years. The fastest ascent, from Plaza de Mulas to the summit, has steadily decreased from 9 hours in 1987 to 5 hours and 45 minutes in 1991 (by a German by the name of Porche!). The fastest descent was by parachute in 1985 when A Steves of the French Air Force came down in 25 minutes. In 1991 and 1992 records were further set for an ascent and descent in one day via the Normal Route and the Polish Glacier route.

In 2002 Frenchman Bruno Sourzac summitted solo via the south face from Plaza Francia in 22 hours.

The hotel at Plaza de Mulas

TREKKER/CLIMBER PROFILES

A wide range of people come to climb Aconcagua.

In general, approximately 11 per cent to 18 per cent are female. Of the low level trekkers the percentage of females increases to 35 per cent. Argentineans make up 25 per cent of climbers and 60 per cent of trekkers. The next country with the largest numbers is from the United States, followed by Germany, Spain, France and the United Kingdom. Climbers from Canada visit more than those from Chile, Switzerland and Japan.

A recent new regulation restricts minors from climbing the mountain. No one under 14 may go any higher than 3100m. A child over 14, but under the age of consent (whatever that age is in their country of origin), requires the written permission of both of their parents, witnessed by a notary.

If they are climbing with one of the parents, then the written permission of the other, again notary witnessed, is required. The forms for such consents may be downloaded from the Mendoza government website.

In Argentina the age of consent is 21, so anyone aged 20 or under needs to complete these forms before they can climb the mountain.

WEATHER

The most predictable aspect of the weather on Aconcagua is its unpredictability. During the summer months it is likely to be very windy all the time. Out of the wind, down in the valleys, the temperature will be as high as 27°C at midday and as low as 3°C at midnight. At top camp the temperature will fall to at least -15°C at night, possibly as low as -30°C. In

Plaza de Mulas under snow

A storm over Aconcagua contrasts with the tranquillity at Horcones

the middle of the day on the summit the temperature could range from as low as -35°C to as high as 10°C.

During the summer on the mountain it will be cold in the morning until the sun shines. After 6pm sunset will fast descend and the temperature will drop sharply within a short period.

An important feature of the weather on Aconcagua is the wind chill factor. When the wind is particularly strong and cold this can have the effect of lowering the temperature, from the leeward side to the wind side, by as much as 15°C.

The region is also subject to El Niño, a summer phenomenon in the southern hemisphere that can dramatically alter the weather. The cold Antarctic waters that flow northwards along the South American coast are deflected to the west. Warmer seas with more evaporation mean heavy rain. In January 1998 Buenos Aires was drenched with 70mm of rain in a few hours, which caused extensive flooding.

El Niño is as likely to cause dry weather as it is wet weather, and there have been periods of extreme drought. In 1998, for instance, on the western side of South America there was no rain during the winter or spring, which led to a severe drought. El Niño tends to occur once every five years, making 2013 and 2018 possible vulnerable years.

The predominant winds in the central Andes come from the west or the southwest. As they rise over the mountains their velocity increases. In summer their precipitation is usually in the form of snow rather than rain. During the day, therefore, winds whip through the valleys. At night ice-cold winds come down from the mountaintops.

35

Aconcagua itself has its own microclimate. The weather can be pleasant in the central Andes at the same time as a storm is raging up on Aconcagua. Electric storms during the summer are not uncommon. Occasionally the weather will produce a mushroom of cloud over the summit, with severe winds and driving snow.

Weather watching is a particular expertise of the local guides, and much of their conversations revolve around this topic. Winds from the south are a sign of good weather; those from the north or the west are not. The guides will know what the normal barometric pressure is at each campsite and they will be alerted by changes in the barometer.

On all of the Andean peaks the daily pattern tends to an early clearance of cloud that may provide clear weather until midday. In the early afternoon the tendency is for the clouds to appear, engulfing the summit by mid- to late afternoon, then clearing again as night falls. Summiting at midday is therefore a good plan.

During the 2001/2 season, in the period from 24 December to 30 December, the wind blew down the Horcones valley from the north. A blizzard greeted new arrivals at Plaza de Mulas on 1 January. Many of them had left Confluencia in T-shirts and shorts, and were caught unawares. Meanwhile, up on the mountain there were no successful summits for five days, and only nine successful attempts in the succeeding two days. Hundreds of climbers went home disappointed. Determined climbers descended to recover, recalling six nights of -26°C.

In early January 2003 there was snow on the summit, and the Canaleta was relatively easy to climb with crampons. Within a few days the snow was gone and the Canaleta scree had returned to its loose nature. The winds whipped up, gusting to over 100km an hour. The wind chill reduced temperatures by 15°C. The severe winds only lasted a few days. When they abated, the weather was ideal for climbing, and the temperature on the summit was in the mid-teens Centigrade.

By 2009 global warming had reduced the volume of snow on the mountain and curtailed the extent of glaciers and penitentes. That January frozen snow on the Canaleta made climbing it easy. Conversely, underfoot conditions on the Polish Glacier were poor. A layer of soft snow covered the ice, so that securing a foothold was often difficult. Tragically these conditions are blamed for the loss of life of three people, all within days of each other in early January 2009.

Climate in Santiago and Mendoza

During the summer it will generally be a little warmer and more humid in Mendoza than across the mountains in Santiago. Whereas there will be virtually no chance of rain during the Santiago summer, in Mendoza the summer season is not only the

TEMPERATURES AND RAINFALL IN SANTIAGO AND MENDOZA

	Max/Min temperature (°C)		Monthly rainfall (mm)	
	Santiago	Mendoza	Santiago	Mendoza
December	28/11	30/15	5	20
January	29/12	32/16	3	29
February	29/12	30/15	3	33
March	27/10	27/13	5	28
April	23/8	23/8	13	13
May	18/6	18/7	64	10
June	14/4	14/3	84	9
July	15/3	14/2	76	8
August	17/4	17/4	56	5
September	19/6	19/7	31	13
October	21/8	21/10	15	17
November	22/9	27/11	8	18

warm season, but also the wet season. A monthly summer rainfall of only 20mm to 30mm is nevertheless extremely small. Santiago has more than double Mendoza's rainfall, but it all falls during the winter.

GETTING THERE

When to go

The climbing season on Aconcagua is from mid-November to mid-March, during the South American summer.

In mid-November it is springtime in South America, but the snow on the Andes is deep, and the weather unpredictable. The various camps are being set up and the *arrieros* (mule handlers) are only coming up from the lowlands. December and January is high season and this is when 80 per cent of climbers come. The weather is best from mid-December to early February. By mid-March the summer has ended and those who serve the climbers are packing up for another year. Once again the incidences of storms in the Andes increase.

At the height of the season the basecamps are crowded, mules are nearly all pre-booked, accommodation at Los Penitentes and Puente del Inca is full, the cost of a permit is high and an additional premium is added to almost everything. On the Normal Route there are many climbers vying for clean snow to melt and sanitation suffers.

To climb outside the designated climbing season nevertheless requires a permit. In order to discourage climbers when there is no emergency rescue, no ranger control and no services

PEAK TREKKING TIMES		
Month	Week	% of all trekkers
November	3	1.0
	4	2.3
December	1	4.0
	2	5.8
	3	10.0
	4	12.6
January	1	14.0
	2	13.0
	3	11.1
	4	8.2
February	1	9.1
	2	5.0
	3	2.3
	4	1.0
March	1	0.5
	2	0.1

on the mountain, the authorities impose a higher than normal rate.

The best balance of avoiding the crowds and advantageous weather is the two weeks before Christmas, or the last week in January and the first week in February. There is a surge of people who want to celebrate Christmas before leaving for the climb. A review of the statistics shows, for some strange reason, a dip in the numbers who arrive in the last week in January.

The table above shows the official figures for the percentage of trekkers that tackle the mountain in particular weeks of the season, calculated by taking an average over many years.

The variation from year to year is not significant.

Mendoza is very busy in late February and early March with wine harvesting. The first week in March is the great wine festival, when the city is filled with visitors. Accommodation will be difficult to procure, and many of those working on Aconcagua may have returned to the lowlands to help with the harvest and join in the festivities. However, if accommodation is secure, the carnival atmosphere can be an exhilarating way to finish an expedition.

The inward journey

The Aconcagua roadhead lies roughly midway along the main road from Mendoza to Santiago. However, as everyone has to obtain a permit in person in Mendoza, this is the most convenient starting point.

International flights do not land in Mendoza. The nearest international airport is Santiago, 35 minutes by aeroplane away, or Buenos Aires, 1½ hours away.

The following airlines operate into Chile and Argentina:
• Aerolineas Argentinas (Argentina's National Airline of Argentina)
• LAN Chile (Chile's National Airline)
• Varig (Brazil's National Airline)
• Iberia (Spain's National Airline)
• American Airlines
• United Airlines, and
• British Airways.

A mule train en route out of Confluencia

It pays to take some time planning your flights and comparing alternative prices. An experienced global travel agent can reduce your flight costs by anything up to a third. Give due attention to the baggage allowance. With all the gear you need you can expect to be carrying over 25kg. Iberia's allowance is 23kgs, whereas British Airways is 46kgs. Airline check-ins in

Europe and North America are more lenient than those in South America, so if you are a few kgs over the right weight you may get a nasty surprise. If you fly via Buenos Aires you will need to change airport there.

Cabin air filtration on long-haul flights differs from airline to airline. The easiest place to pick up an infection is on an air flight and then the altitude on the climb has a way of seeking out any minor ailments and exacerbating them. A mild chest infection can rise to pneumonia quite easily on the mountain.

Sao Paulo, in Brazil, is a common stopover en route from Europe. The flight from Sao Paulo or Madrid to Santiago circles around Aconcagua before descending to land. The view from the aeroplane can be quite spectacular – so try for a seat on the right-hand side of the plane. Flying from Buenos Aires to Mendoza, conversely, provides no view of the Andes.

Some parties land in Santiago, then travel by bus over the Andes to Mendoza, stopping off to look at the mountain en route, and returning to the Andes after a day or so in Mendoza. The road journey is a round trip of 540km, which can be rather tedious, especially if all it achieves is a brief look at the mountain. A stop to trek up to the statue of Christ the Redeemer, or to watch river rafting, would be a welcome break.

Visas, passports and permits

Visas are not required from any Western or first world country to enter either Chile or Argentina. For Chile visas are required from Russia, a number of Central American countries, Korea and former communist countries. In both countries the traveller's passport must have at least six months

remaining, and generally entry to the country is restricted to 90 days.

There are rumours that Argentina may move to protect the livelihood of its guides by forbidding foreign guides from operating in the country. If you are leading a group it may be worth considering that you are not working, but on holiday too.

At the land border crossing expect to be delayed for some time whilst passports and luggage are checked. Expect also to pay a few dollars to a bureaucratic official who may insist on a thorough luggage examination. This petty corruption is more likely on the Argentinean side than on the Chilean side.

Before entering Aconcagua Provincial Park you must have a permit and permits are issued in Mendoza, at the Subsecretario de Turismo. You have to present yourself in person, fill in forms and show your passport. The office is located in the Tourist Office building on Avenida San Martin, near Garibaldi (on the same side of the street,

COSTS OF PERMITS FOR ACONCAGUA NATIONAL PARK (2008/9)					
Season	Dates	Climbing	Long trek	Short trek	Day visit
	Max days in park:	20	7	3	1
High	15 Dec–31 Jan	1500 pesos	330 pesos	170 pesos	60 pesos
Medium	1 Dec–14 Dec				
	1 Feb–20 Feb	1000 pesos	220 pesos	150 pesos	60 pesos
Low	15–30 Nov				
	21 Mar–15 Mar	500 pesos	220 pesos	150 pesos	60 pesos
Winter	All except above	2000 pesos			

and close to MacDonald's) and the procedure is a little complex.

In the Aconcagua permit office on the first floor you first of all get a small payment form. You take this outside and find a *pago facil*. These private payment centres (rather insignificant premises) handle payments for all types of services – telephone, water, electricity. Some double as internet offices. You can jump the queue there, because Aconcagua payments are priority. With your payment slip you return to the permit office, fill in the other forms and present your passport.

The rates quoted in the table opposite are for foreigners. Argentineans pay approximately a third of this. When rates were fixed for 2008/9 the exchange rate was 3.45 pesos to the dollar.

Permits are issued Mondays to Fridays from 8am to 6pm, and on Saturdays and Sundays from 9am to 1pm. The centre is closed on Christmas Day and New Year's Day.

At the park entrance the permit must be shown and passports checked (Horcones Valley side only – the first check on the Vacas Valley is at Pampa de Leñas). Each trekker is issued with a refuse sack, which must be brought back out, full. Out-of-season permits are the same cost as high season permits. Daily permits can be purchased at the Horcones ranger station.

If you stay longer in the park than the designated number of days you will be charged a further full permit cost. If you purchase a trekking permit

The park ranger hands out numbered refuse sacks at Pampa de Leñas

and climb higher than basecamp you will be faced with a fine of two times the ascent permit cost (3000 pesos)

Leave no Trace policy
The park authorities have become very strict on minimising interference with the environment, on keeping the park clean and controlling waste. A major review and policy statement was produced in 2007, which introduction on-the-spot fines for various offences.

Up to 500 pesos may be imposed for:
• not using designated toilets
• burning native wood, or starting fires outside of designated areas
• burning garbage or polluting rivers
• bringing domestic animals, plants or exotic animals into the park.

41

Up to 1000 pesos may be imposed for:

- throwing garbage about
- loss of the prescribed refuse sack
- damaging wildlife or plants.

Rangers are under orders to be proactive in the camps. They will severely reprimand those urinating in any place other than the designated toilets; they will point out garbage or material that may be susceptible to being blown away.

PREPARATIONS

Motivation

To climb a mountain such as Aconcagua is a major life commitment, one to be taken most seriously. Once that decision is made you must realise that there will be multiple decisions that you must make, many things to do and numerous checklists to go through to ensure the success of the mission. Failure to attend to one of these may be the difference between success and failure.

You are going to have to prepare your body physically and your mind psychologically. You will need to ensure that you have all the necessary and correct equipment. When you are on the mountain you will need to take care to eat the right foods, drink adequate water and look after your other bodily needs.

If you set out assuming that someone else is going to take care of any of these essentials you have started off badly.

Crampons, double plastic boots and down jacket are essential

Teamwork

You will not achieve this particular goal on your own, so you have to commit to being part of a team or a partnership. That has to be a full commitment on both sides. You are likely on summit day to be paired, so choose your partner carefully. They must have similar abilities to you. Build a good relationship with your guide if you have hired one. If you are not part of a group team up with a good climber and build a rapport with them.

When it comes to the crunch on summit day, you must be prepared to turn around to assist your team or partner, and you must be confident that they would do the same for you.

Essential gear

Down in Mendoza or Santiago, before and after the climb, shorts, T-shirts and light summer clothing will be the appropriate attire. This is the middle of summer. Even at night the temperature will be in the low twenties. The summer months in Mendoza may produce a rare downpour, but this is so rare as to be ignored.

For the walk in to basecamp shorts and T-shirts will again be appropriate, but warmer clothing and waterproofs should be in the rucksacks. Sun protection during the two to three-day walk should not be underestimated. The searing sun on your back will be relentless. A cool full-sleeve dry flow top and similar trousers may be more appropriate than a vest and shorts as sun protection.

Your summer clothing can be stored at basecamp. It will be warm in the middle of the day but the temperatures in the morning and afternoon will require warmer clothing.

A number of items of non-standard gear are required on Aconcagua:
- double plastic boots
- down jacket
- crampons
- ice axe
- harness
- -18°C sleeping bag
- sleeping mattress
- pee bottle
- a length of 9mm rope 15m long
- 8 lithium disposable hand warmers.

A down jacket is an essential item of clothing for the long cold evenings at basecamp and above. The down jacket will likely be slept in to supplement the -18°C sleeping bag at the top camp.

Similarly double plastic boots are essential above basecamp. Leather boots will freeze. There are varieties of insulated leather boots that will be adequate at basecamp and the lower camps. This is provided that the boots are taken into the tent at night and that they are left in the sun in the morning to thaw.

However, for the top camps there is no substitute for the double plastics. Virtually every climber on Aconcagua wears them. Indeed some walk in from the roadhead in the double plastics, dispensing with the weight of

Be prepared for heavy snow

TIPS FOR MINIMISING YOUR GEAR

- At basecamp there will be ample time to wash clothes, and the drying conditions will be ideal. Even heavy woollen socks will dry under the sun and wind in a few hours.
- High on the mountain sweat is not an issue. Few will have the energy or inclination to brave the cold to change regularly.
- If crampons and ice axes are items that must be acquired then check out the various weights. Manufacturers, such as Camp and Cassin, produce lightweight gear.
- Western airlines tend to have a lenient approach to excess baggage. This is not the custom in South America. At over $33 per excess kilo one could be faced with a hefty bill on the home journey.

trekking boots. The rangers now list double plastic boots and crampons as compulsory above the basecamps.

As you ascend to the higher camps it is much colder and windier. Most climbers only bring the double plastics. You will be wearing your inner boots during the night at top camp. Wind bloc fleeces are essential, but as soon as the sun sets you will need your down jacket.

For summit day be prepared to set off in the dark when the temperature will be at least -10°C, and the chill

SURVIVAL TIP

A satchel that slips into the top of the rucksack, and that can take your precious items, such as passport, airline ticket, camera, is most convenient. Around the city and the campsites it is better than an awkward rucksack.

factor from the wind will decrease the temperature significantly. As the day progresses the temperature will rise, so that a layering system for all parts of the body should be automatic, including a balaclava and wool hat, several layers of gloves and so on. The morning temperature may be so severe you will have to wear your down jacket until dawn. Small lithium disposable hand warmers, slipped into the palm of the glove can be very effective on a cold morning.

The ice axe, harness and crampons may only be required for summit day. Some guides will dispense with a harness, because they can put together an adequate makeshift harness from a length of rope. The pee bottle (with funnel for ladies) is required so that you don't need to get out of your tent at the higher altitude.

The ground surface on the mountain is stony. In all the campsites tents will be pitched on this stony ground,

Wading through the Relinchos River

too hard to pierce with timber or steel pegs. Tents will be held down with boulders (which are plentiful). Mattresses to alleviate the uneven, rough surface are a necessity.

Items of standard gear include

• a pair of walking sticks
• category 4 sunglasses (two pairs)
• walking boots
• a day back-pack (40 litres) and a large rucksack (80 litres)
• sun hats
• bandanas, and
• gaiters to keep snow out of boots.

The likelihood is that only the large rucksack will be taken above basecamp. Daypacks are not big enough for carrying loads from camp to camp, and bringing the daypack for summit day may be seen as a luxury. The large rucksack is the one therefore that will be used on summit day. So, if it's your style is to have many attachments to the final assault rucksack it should be made ready at basecamp. In particular the rucksack must have attachments for an ice axe, crampons and walking sticks.

A mule will carry the gear into basecamp. The mule will not stop at the intermediate camps in the valley approach, so that the mattress and sleeping bag will have to be carried in the day backpack. A sturdy gear bag is recommended. It will suffer considerable abuse on the back of a mule.

On the valley approaches rivers have to be crossed. There are two bridges in the Horcones valley and one in the Vacas Valley where the river is deep, but it is still necessary to cross a number of times over the shallower sections. Gore-Tex boots and the pair

SURVIVAL TIP
If you keep a diary, you should note that ballpoint pens are very susceptible to freezing at high altitude. Keep them warm. Fountain pens are less so, but bring a pencil, just in case.

of walking sticks will be invaluable. In the Vacas Valley it is necessary to wade, jump or be carried across the river a number of times. A pair of plimsoles or running shoes may well be worthwhile for these crossings, because the water is ice cold and the riverbed uneven.

The severe winds in the valleys whip up the dust. Bandanas or neckerchiefs are good protection against driving dust and sand.

The medical kit
There are a few items that may not be standard that should be included in the medical bag along with your standard first-aid kit.
• Sun protection factor 50 or better will be required high up the mountain, and factor 20 for the valley approach.
• The wind will dry and chaff the lips. You will need cream protection and repair. Lip healing ointment is highly sought after at the roadhead as climbers recover from their summit attempts.
• Bowel-release and bowel-stop pills should be included.

• Facial wipes will prevent you from getting too dirty and smelly where water is scarce or stripping off is not an option.

The altitude has differing affects on people and strangely seems to affect young people more. Headaches, feelings of nausea and sickness are common and few will escape without some discomfort.

There is a diversity of opinion on the use of Diamox (medical name acetazolamide). It was originally prescribed for glaucoma and has been found effective in alleviating altitude sickness. The medication generally comes in 250mg tablets. A typical dose is half a tablet twice daily.

Medical opinion is that it can do no harm. It has even been suggested that doubling or tripling the dose is better, but Diamox has side effects. It causes tingling of the tips of the fingers and toes (which should not be misinterpreted as frostbite in the hallucinationary periods on summit day!). A secondary side effect is tenderness in the fingers and toes that can linger for a few weeks after medication has ceased. It also increases dehydration and, on an arid mountain like Aconcagua, this is a significant issue.

The consumption of copious amounts of liquid is most important at high altitude. Four to five litres of water a day should be regarded as a minimum. Very often simply the immediate drinking of a litre of water can dispel a headache or a nausea attack. Guides will recommend that people taking

Stretching the legs at Los Penitentes

Diamox should aim for six litres a day.

Liquids can be spread between water, tea or coffee, juices, soups and so on. Of course, the more you drink the more your need to urinate. This is not a problem during the day, but at night dressing up to go out in the cold air is not to be recommended – hence the need for a pee bottle. Experience has shown that the pee bottle should be at least 1½ litres, or alternatively two one-litre bottles, and that it should have a wide brim. Collapsible pee bottles are most useful. Pee bottles of the same shape and size as drink bottles are obviously not a good idea.

Other preparations

Aconcagua is a difficult mountain and hence requires considerable preparation.

- A superior level of fitness is essential to success. Summit day requires stamina and endurance – in fact pure, brute doggedness. Spurts of training will obviously be inferior to long bouts in the hills, on the road or in the gym.
- You must also be used to, and able to deal with, severe cold. The best way to be prepared for the cold is to have a fit body that has trained regularly in cold and wind chilled conditions.
- Feet do not break in double plastic boots – the boots break in the feet. Your feet should be accustomed to the rigidity of the boots, especially at the heels and ankles.
- Fitting, removing and refitting crampons should be second nature. On summit day you may need to put them on in the dark, so learn to strap them tight.
- There will be a minor degree of rope work, so that familiarity with knots and hooking up are important.

47

Getting ready for summit day should start before the expedition begins, and should be reassessed at basecamp. Have a checklist of clothing and gear, from head to feet. A simple deficiency that may not matter elsewhere could be the difference between summiting and failure. What will you eat? Don't rely on someone handing you a suitable package for the day, or being able to put a suitable package together.

Consider bringing a container from home with food that is non-perishable, can be eaten if frozen and does not require excessive chewing. The kind of high-calorie drinks often prescribed for cancer patients are a meal equivalent. Jelly babies, mint chocolate and the like are nourishing and require little effort to eat. But remember that foodstuffs such as cheese, fruit and cereals can not be taken into Chile.

These are perhaps the special requirements of Aconcagua. Spending two to three weeks in a tent, living out of a rucksack, caring for one's feet, reading, eating and stumbling around by head torch are discomforts that can be learned.

ACCLIMATISATION

Getting used to thin air
Perhaps the most important element in a successful expedition on such a high mountain is acclimatisation. The longer one spends either at basecamp

and the lower camps or at other high elevations the better one will be at high altitude.

Acclimatising on another mountain, such as Vallecitos or El Plomo, can be interesting but will involve additional organisation, time and expense that you may not want to be burdened with. Trekking in and around the provincial park is an easy alternative. Professional guiding companies, recognising the great advantage of pre-acclimatisation, are now offering packages of two peaks in the Andes, such Vallecitos–Aconcagua or El Plomo–Aconcagua.

As soon as you get off the bus at Los Penitentes or Puente del Inca the thin air is apparent. Breathlessness follows even minor degrees of physical effort. It takes time to become accustomed to this. A slow build-up is recommended. Early exertions can lead to nausea and sickness. However, there is equally little point in being too careful or taking things too easy. You must gauge how your own body is being affected and if exertions are showing no ill effects then you should push yourself a little further.

At the permit office there is an excellent booklet available free of charge that provides information on the provincial park. Contained in the booklet is a guide to altitude ailments. This awards points for medical/physical conditions and recommends appropriate treatment (see box opposite).

BREAKFAST AT LOS PENITENTES

When the early bustle of climbers at the Hotel had subsided there were two British climbers remaining. Both had been forced to abandon their climb prematurely.

Alan from Leeds, who was in his forties and had been to an altitude of 3600m before coming to Aconcagua, had come down from Camp Canada suffering from pulmonary oedema. His breakfast companion, Richard from Reading, was a little younger. He had been brought down from Nido de Condores with cerebral oedema. They both described their experiences.

Alan had no difficulty on his initial visit to Camp Canada. It was when the team moved there to sleep that he found breathing difficult. He was sick and had chronic diarrhoea. When he arrived down at Plaza de Mulas the doctor recorded his saturated oxygen at only 63% and ordered him airlifted out immediately. He recounted how the pilot had great difficulty with the helicopter in the wind, trying to avoid hitting the sides of the valley. Alan had had a bad night in Los Penitentes and was waiting for transport down to Mendoza.

Richard, on the other hand, had made a complete recovery, had eaten dinner the night before and was tucking into a hearty breakfast. His transport out from Plaza de Mulas was by mule.

DEALING WITH ALTITUDE SICKNESS

Symptoms
- Headache, nausea, loss of appetite and dizziness are allotted *1 point*.
- Vomiting and headaches that are resistant to aspirin/paracetamol are allotted *2 points*.
- Shortness of breath at rest, abnormal fatigue and a low urine volume are allotted *3 points*.

Recommended treatment
- For up to 3 points aspirin or paracetamol is the recommended treatment, with plenty of water.
- From 3 to 6 points it is recommended that ascending ceases, that the climber rests, drinks and takes paracetamol/aspirin, again with copious amounts of water.
- Above 6 points the climber is advised to descend.

Saturated oxygen

As part of its services in policing the Aconcagua provincial park the local government in Mendoza sponsors medical tents at Plaza de Mulas and Plaza Argentina where climbers are invited to be checked before they ascend.

The most important aspect of this check is one's saturated oxygen level. This is normally done with a small pulse oximeter. The device is placed over the index finger. It transmits red and infrared light through the finger and detects fluctuating signals caused by blood flow. The ratio of the fluctuation of the red and infrared light signals is used to calculate the blood oxygen saturation ($\%SPO_2$).

Haemoglobin molecules in the blood carry oxygen. For a healthy person at rest at sea level the percentage of haemoglobin molecules that carry oxygen could, theoretically, be as high as 100 per cent, but, in practice, it is a little less than this. As you climb it is natural for some of the molecules not to carry oxygen. However, the higher the number that do carry oxygen the better.

TARGET SPO_2 LEVELS	
Altitude (m)	Target $\%SPO_2$
zero	99
1500	93
2000	92
4000	88
5000	83
6000	77

At the basecamps, where the altitude is approximately 4250m, a $\%SPO_2$ in the upper 80s is desirable, and some will register over 90. A count under 80 will generally be accompanied by advice to stay at basecamp, relax and drink. A count of less than 70 may come with a recommendation, or indeed an order, to descend.

Cold acclimatisation

If you are an experienced climber you will have been in cold situations on mountains before. You will be aware how far you may allow your hands and feet to suffer cold, knowing that they will eventually return to normal albeit with a sharp pain. You will need

The doctor checks saturated oxygen at Plaza Argentina

An expedition team at the Horcones trail head

this experience for Aconcagua so that you can tell when you are within your limits and when you have overstepped the mark. You should be able to recognise, when your fingers and toes are numb, that they will return to normal eventually and that this will be accompanied by this sharp pain. You will be experienced enough to know that if that situation does not right itself then you must take measures to remedy the situation (see later under 'Summit day' and 'Dealing with Problems').

GUIDES AND MULES

Guides and their necessity

With only the simple word Aconcagua search engines on the internet will display countless companies and individuals who provide guided tours up the mountain. You have the choice of joining a group in your own country, joining a group in Mendoza organised by local Argentineans, or simply going solo.

There is no requirement to hire a guide, and a significant number of climbers and trekkers opt to travel unaccompanied. Mules can be hired on an individual basis at the road-head, or in advance through the mule companies. At Confluencia, and Plaza de Mulas there are restaurants (fairly limited and basic). At Plaza de Mulas there is even a hotel, with full shower, toilet, restaurant, international telephone link. However, there are no shops on the mountain, so that all provisions for the higher camps must be taken.

There are great advantages in hiring a local guide, or joining a locally-organised group. The guides know the mountain, speak the language, and

High mountain guides Pablo Reguera and Mauricio Fernandez

most important, can read the weather. When mini crises arise, as they often do, a local guide's help can be invaluable. For the local guide the mountain is his livelihood; guiding is his profession. They will have summitted many times. Altitude will have little effect on them. The various guides know one another, so that when one runs out of an essential commodity he knows that he can get help.

Local guides will know the medical doctor on duty, and will know how to raise him in an emergency. If you climb unguided you need to be be reasonably confident that altitude will not cause a crisis for you. Guides will help unguided travellers in an emergency, but with a degree of reluctance. Your guide will discourage you from inviting unguided travellers to accompany the trek, no matter how companionable they are.

The tour operators on the mountain provide toilet facilities for their clients. This is a much more convenient service than collecting one's waste and carrying it in one's refuse sack or trying to purchase latrine facilities at the basecamp and above.

A word of warning: if it is proposed to hire a guide then pick a guide carefully. A bad guide may be worse than no guide.

Choosing a guide or expedition organiser

A licensed guide in Argentina must undergo two periods of training, each 20 weeks long, one during the summer and the other during the winter. These guides will have a comprehensive medical kit, including stethoscope, syringes and bandages.

For the 2007/8 season the Mendoza Government published

the list of its 111 approved guides. Obviously, with so many climbers there are not enough qualified guides to serve them.

The larger operators have permanent compounds at the main campsites. When you arrive with the guide the tents are already in place, inside an enclosure that includes the mess tents. Others may have to clear stones and perch wherever there is space available.

With guides and with permanent compounds the premier operators can take a party up one route and return a different route. They will also tailor their service to the traveller's requirements. A popular service that is available is to arrange pick-up from the airport, hotel in Mendoza, transportation to and from the mountain, and a mule service, but no mountain guide.

In selecting a guide the following obvious questions should be asked.

- How many days are allowed to the summit? Are there any spare days? This is most important. Some guides have little motivation to take climbers to the summit. They have the attitude that the climber may accept that they were not capable or ready, when, in fact, they were given inadequate time by the guide to acclimatise.
- What is the ratio of guides to trekkers? A ratio of one guide for every three trekkers should be regarded as a minimum, especially for summit day. There

TREKKING COMPANIES	
Company	% Climbers with each (2008/9)
Inka	16%
Grajales	15%
Aymara	12%
Campo Base	10%
Puquios	10%
Aconcagua Express	7%

must be adequate guides to bring down people who cannot go on.
- Are the guides licensed?
- How many times has the guide(s) summitted?
- What medical equipment will the guide have – Diamox, saturated oxygen monitor, bowel control tablets, syringes and so on?
- Will the guide have a radio that can raise basecamp and the doctor?
- What food will be provided – normally, and on summit day?
- What is the hotel accommodation in Mendoza – single or double and what standard?
- Tents – how many to a tent and how big are the tents?
- What are the extra costs for any special arrangements – for instance, going up one route and returning by a different route or visiting the Christ the Redeemer Statue or Plaza Francia for acclimatisation?

Some operators, advertising on the internet, offer a package that takes 15 days. This is much too optimistic for those who have no acclimatisation. The inevitable result may be that the summit attempt fails, or that the operator claims an extra premium if the expedition time is extended.

The table on the previous page shows the breakdown of climbers using the companies that were providing services to clients during the 2007/8 season. That season Inka had an equal presence at both Plaza de Mulas and Plaza Argentina. The main emphasis with Inka was on fully organised and guided expeditions. Grajales would tend to attract more of the clients who were seeking basic services, possibly without guides. Grajales featured very little at Plaza de Mulas, but had a strong presence at Plaza Argentina. Campo Base had no presence at Plaza de Mulas, and concentrated on treks into Confluencia. Puquios was formally known as Rudy Parra.

The duration of the typical itinerary for the Vacas Valley Route shown in the box below should be regarded

TYPICAL ITINERARY FOR THE VACAS VALLEY ROUTE	
Day 1	Arrive Mendoza
Day 2	Obtain permit and travel to Puente del Inca
Day 3	Start Trek: Punta de Vacas to Pampa de Leñas
Day 4	Pampa de Leñas to Casa Piedra
Day 5	Casa Piedra to Plaza Argentina
Day 6	Rest Day
Day 7	Visit Camp 1
Day 8	Rest Day
Day 9	Move to Camp 1
Day 10	Visit Camp 2
Day 11	Rest Day
Day 12	Move to Camp 2
Day 13	Rest Day
Day 14	Move to Rocas Blancas
Day 15	Summit Day
Day 16	Spare Day
Day 17	Descend to Basecamp
Day 18	Basecamp to Intermediate Camp
Day 19	Intermediate Camp to Roadhead
Day 20	Transport to Santiago or Mendoza
Day 21	Flight home

A BETTER ITINERARY USING THE NORMAL ROUTE

Day 1	Arrive Mendoza
Day 2	Obtain Permits. Travel to Vallecitos 2900m
Day 3	Short acclimatisation treks in Vallecitos (rope and crampon trials)
Day 4	Short acclimatisation treks in Vallecitos 2980m
Day 5	Trek to Piedra Grande in Vallecitos 3500m
Day 6	Trek to El Salto 4200m
Day 7	Trek to La Hoyada 4500m
Day 8	Summit day to Vallecitos 5770m
Day 9	Return to Vallecitos centre
Day 10	Travel to Los Penitentes and make ready for Aconcagua
Day 11	Walk in to Confluencia 3440m
Day 12	Walk to Plaza de Mulas 4350m
Day 13	Rest Day
Day 14	Move to Camp Canada 4900m
Day 15	Move to Nido de Condores 5350m
Day 16	Rest Day
Day 17	Move to Berlin 5850m
Day 18	Summit Day and return to Berlin
Day 19	Spare Day
Day 20	Return to Plaza de Mulas
Day 21	Return to Penitentes
Day 22	Return to Mendoza
Day 23	Flight home

as a minimum for those who are not acclimatised. An extra day at Puente del Inca to go to the statue of Christ the Redeemer, and another around Day 10, will assist with acclimatisation.

A better plan, better use of time and money, with acclimatisation on another mountain, is set out in the second box. You will have tested yourself before the big event. If you do not succeed in scaling Vallecitos it is no loss because it was not your main goal.

Without a guide

Well-prepared seasoned travellers may want to climb the mountain without a guide, some even without a mule, and there is no restriction on them so doing. In fact travelling alone can have many benefits – it reduces costs significantly, you eat what and when you want, you are not hampered by the inability or pace of fellow travellers.

At the permit office a question on the application form will ask about a guide but this can be ignored. There will be no cross examination on your skill or abilities. At the campsites that have rangers on duty you will have to present your permit and possibly also your passport.

On the road and in the mountain parks there are no great dangers, no history of highwaymen and the locals are usually very friendly. Language will be a barrier, but not an insurmountable one.

It will be most important that a detailed checklist is made of essential items for the trek. On the mountain cooked food can be purchased at the basecamps, but otherwise there will be no means of acquiring foodstuffs or fuel except through barter with others.

The Arreiros

The men who handle the mules on Aconcagua are known as *arrieros*. Some work for the big mule operators, but most are freelance agents hired on a weekly basis. Tremendously loyal to each other and their trade, they are all from the plains of Argentina, where they spend the winters herding cattle.

Some will consider them cruel to the mules they handle. However, in the author's experience they are a hard-working group of men with a wonderful sense of humour. Mules are stubborn animals that have to be continually controlled. A mule cannot be coaxed into action. Mules in the mountains are relatively valuable – about the same value as a horse. Whereas a horse has to be fed in these arid lands, a mule will generally fend

MATE

Mate is South American tea. Made from a chopped up grassy herb and hot water it is drunk from a small vessel, or gourd, through a metal filter, or bombilla. The grass, or *yerba mate*, is grown in northern Argentina, southern Paraguay and Bolivia. Packed in one kilo bags it contains natural minerals and vitamins.

The custom of mate is popular in southern Brazil, Peru and Uruguay and is a national obsession in Argentina. Only a little is consumed in Chile.

When mate is taken one person will be in control. They will prepare the initial mixture, taste it and pass it around. The gourd will always be passed back to the controller. To pass it directly to someone else is impolite. The taste is very bitter, but many add sugar to reduce this bitterness. A gourd filling will last from ten to thirty water toppings. The advent of hot water flasks has provided a great new convenience to the taking of mate.

Mate is now available in tea-bag format, and in being sold all over the world. It is to be hoped that it will not entirely replace the traditional custom of drinking mate in a group with a common gourd.

Mule stop at Plaza de Mulas

for itself, eating almost anything. There is a shortage of donkeys in Argentina, so that mules are becoming scarce.

The arrieros carry their *mate* (see box) in a satchel that is strewn across the horse. The *yerba mate* will be on one side, possibly with a separate pouch for sugar, and the gourd and bombilla on the other side. Their diet is meat, and plenty of it, cooked on an open fire, eaten, fat and all, with a large sharp knife that they carry in a pouch at their back.

The first arriero to serve on Aconcagua was called Pasten. He assisted both Gussfeldt and later Fitzgerald in their expeditions. One of his descendants works today as an arriero on the mountain.

Hiring mules

Mules can be hired at the roadhead or at the basecamps. It is generally the custom to contract for a round trip from the roadhead to basecamp and back. Prices will vary considerably.

A mule should take no more than 60kgs, 30kgs on each side, and the mule companies may require special rates for loads that do not fit this arrangement. The arrieros jealously reserve the right to decide how loads are distributed, and how they are secured.

An initial rate will be sought for the first mule, and half of this for the next two mules. One arriero can drive no more than three mules, so the cost of the fourth mule may revert to the higher price, the fifth and sixth the lower price, and so on. These rules are not always adhered to, however. You won't know what other arrangements the mule company is making, so that, where you have paid for, say, two mules, in fact your shipment may be part of an enormous mule train.

View of Aconcagua up the Relinchos Valley

PART 1
THE ASCENT OF ACONCAGUA

MENDOZA TO PUENTE DEL INCA

Mendoza, at an elevation of 700m, is a bustling, relatively modern city of over one million inhabitants. Founded in the mid-16th century as a province of Santiago in Chile (and named after the then Captain General of Chile), Mendoza was virtually destroyed by the worst earthquake in South American history in 1861. The city was quickly rebuilt, with wide, tree-lined streets, a central plaza and four satellite plazas (named after the countries that helped in the rebuilding).

The French planner laid the modern city out in a grid pattern. Each street has a grass margin with trees separating the footpath from the road.

In this margin there is a deep trench that conveys water, coming down from the Andes, to irrigate the trees.

Mendoza is the centre of winemaking in Argentina, and the Mendocinos have been making wine since the city was founded. Over 70 per cent of Argentina's wines are produced in Mendoza province, and the majority of the many visitors each year come on wine trips, visiting bodegas in and around Mendoza.

Maps of the city are available at every hotel reception. Essentially it is laid out on an (almost) north–south axis. The main artery, from the airport south through the city and out towards Chile/Aconcagua/Tupungato,

Mendocinos relax in the evening at Plaza Independencia

Central Mendoza

is Av San Martin. The Andes mountains are the second most important attraction of Mendoza for visitors, but only a small proportion come for Aconcagua.

The city is compact, and most places can be reached on foot. It is user friendly and nearly impossible to get lost. There is a strong police presence, many patrolling on bicycles.

The water from the Andes is fundamental to the economy and survival of Mendoza. The main river, Rio Mendoza, is dammed at Potrerillos, where much of the solids settle out. From here it is controlled to irrigate the vineyards, the agricultural lands, city trees and parks. Drinking water is taken from the Rio Blanco below Vallecitos and piped separately to the city. White water rafting (and kayaking) is growing in popularity year by year, and the fast-flowing Mendoza river above Potrerillos is ideal for this activity.

For the mountaineer the city has all the necessary facilities. Some of the best gear shops in the world are here, although the costs are no longer low, and you can also hire gear. Supermarkets within the city and on the outskirts sell food suitable for camping. Internet cafés abound. Post offices (*correos*) and businesses offering the use of telephones (*locutorios*) are alternative, good value options.

Changing money and paying for things

If you are coming from the euro or sterling zones it is better to buy American dollars before you travel, as you will get a better deal than by changing your euros or sterling here. Traveller's cheques lose a significant percentage of their value when changed locally.

Avoid changing any money at the airport, as the rates are poor. In January 2009, the best rate for buying pesos was at 3.45 to the $US, and the rate for the euro was 4.55 (when the official exchange rate was 1.38$ = 1). At that time, the difference between the rate you could get at the airport and the rate at a *casa de cambio* was 14 per cent. Casas de Cambio are located in the vicinity of the tourist office and permit centre and you will need your passport to change foreign currencies.

Buying provisions

The supermarkets of Mendoza are excellent sources of food for the mountain, but not all stock the specialist items that climbers need. There are two Carrefours, for instance, one in the centre of the city on Belgrano, the second on Las Heras.

The most popular form of cooking is using liquid paraffin from a pressurised bottle. This is cheap and transferable, and likely to be one of the heaviest loads you carry. Standard gas canisters are also readily available.

The following tips may be helpful as you stock up for your trip.

- The water available on the mountain comes from melted snow and ice, and contains no minerals or nutrients. Supplements, in the form of flavoured sachets, can provide these ingredients and are widely available.

- Powdered food, such as egg, semolina, milk and potato, is a good and palatable form of food that is easily prepared, although powdered egg is not easy to find.

Fruit for sale by the roadside

- Tea bags, coffee, sugar, soup and the like are freely available. Tea or flavoured herbal mixes may be less harsh on the stomach than coffee, particularly taken in large quantities.

- Bags of muesli and breakfast cereals, including porridge, are popular. Many shops sell an array of nuts that can be added to your muesli.

- Argentinean fruit and vegetables are wonderful. Oranges and grapefruits are relatively large, but not easily damaged, and provide a welcome source of juice. The local tomatoes are particularly large and succulent. A dish of tomatoes and onions, sprinkled with olive oil and a herb-garlic pepper, is quick and easy to prepare. Fruit and vegetables, however, must be protected from frost. Canned forms are not as nourishing or appetising, and are heavier, but last longer.

- Argentina and Chile produce high quality beef and lamb. Getting meat up to basecamp requires an insulated cooler, as there is no traffic in live fowl or animals. Tinned meat is the alternative (available in the smaller shops).

- Specialised boil-in-the-bag meals are not easy to find, and ready-meals are of little use without a microwave. Salami and cheese are great for lunch, and can last the whole expedition if protected.

Casa de Fader, where Fernando Fader's paintings are housed

THE ROAD TO PUENTE DEL INCA

There are three roads out of Mendoza going south towards Chile, Aconcagua and Tupungato. The fastest is the motorway (*autopista*). The most interesting – but also the slowest – is the old route through the vineyards, via the suburb of Lujan. Of further interest along this route is the house of Fernando Fader, the great Mendocino artist whose impressionist style made him world famous.

The long-distance public buses that travel between Santiago and Mendoza are of excellent quality and are relatively inexpensive. The buses from Mendoza stop at the town of Uspallata, an interesting town at an elevation of 1850m. The town was formerly a centre for iron-ore smelting, manufacturing cannonballs for the army that swept down into Chile to defeat the Spanish in 1818. In recent times the area became famous

as the location for the making of the film *Seven Years in Tibet*.

There is a road out of Uspallata to the east, not the old road to Mendoza, but another dirt track road south of it. This road leads to The Rock of the Seven Colours, an unusual volcanic landscape, with colours ranging from white to yellow to purple.

On the approach to Uspallata there is a busy restaurant on the right-hand side, 2km from the village centre. This is Estancia Elias, the best place to eat between Mendoza and Aconcagua. Their *parilla* is particularly good.

Buses do not stop, unless prearranged, at Los Penitentes, Punta de Vacas or Puente del Inca, but it is possible to embark and disembark at Las Cuevas. The cost of a bus ride from the border to either Mendoza or Santiago should be no more than a few dollars. The payment will, almost certainly, go

63

The ski resort of Los Penitentes with Tolosa mountain in the background

directly into the pockets of the driver and courier, so a little bargaining may be required.

Mendoza–Santiago disused railway

The Mendoza–Santiago Railway is a most interesting feature of the landscape that runs parallel to the road all the way from city to city. It was built between 1890 and 1920 and its scale is an indication of the wealth in the region during that period. There are numerous tunnels and bridges. All of the sleepers on the Argentinean side are timber, but the Chileans opted for steel sleepers in the mountains on their side.

When it opened in the 1920s it carried both goods and passengers along the 350km journey. Subject to regular rockslides and subsidence the railway required costly maintenance.

At Las Cuevas, for instance, the enormous boulders on the line that rolled down in an avalanche are testament to this. Eventually the railway that took so much effort to construct was allowed to fall into disrepair and was closed permanently in the 1980s. There were allegations at the time that the Chilean dictator, Pinochet, was involved in the largest trucking company, and that this made the decision easier.

Nowadays the drone of juggernauts and buses has replaced the noise of steam. In recent times estimates have been prepared to restore the railway, but the one billion dollar project has stalled. The truckers are a powerful political force.

Los Penitentes

Los Penitentes is the most popular stop for climbers. It is a ski resort with a cable car and a number of hotels. During the summer only one or two establishments are open.

Los Penitentes is at an elevation of 2580m, so the effects of altitude will begin here for those who are not acclimatised. A good policy is to walk around, even if only to go up and down the road, to start the acclimatisation process.

Southeast of Los Penitentes lies Punta de Vacas. This is essentially an army base that caters for long-distance trucks. It has no shop or hotel.

Back towards Punta de Vacas there is a little natural history museum built out of the ruins of an old railway structure. The enthusiastic owner (who speaks not a word of English) has a makeshift array of pulleys and pumps that simulate tectonic plate movement, earthquakes and volcanic action. Well worth the $US1 entry.

From Los Penitentes, if you walk back far enough towards Punta de Vacas, at a bend in the road there is a clear view of Tupungato.

Between Los Penitentes and Puente del Inca is the Andinistas Graveyard. Many of those buried in the graveyard died on Aconcagua. This is a relatively short walk from Los Penitentes, and one that many climbers take.

Puente del Inca

It would be most unfortunate for the traveller to come to Aconcagua and not experience Puente del Inca. The natural wonder of the bridge and its thermal waters should not be missed.

Puente del Inca is a better, less expensive, place to stay than Los Penitentes. It is closer to the Horcones road head and is full of life. By contrast,

The Andinista graveyard

the juggernauts do not even change gear when going through Los Penitentes.

The village takes its name from the natural bridge over the River Las Cuevas. Only 50m from the main road, the bridge is accessed on foot via a wide lane that has souvenir stalls on either side. The banks of the river are coloured a bright orange by the sulphur from the hot springs. Notices by the bridge display how it was formed – an ice bridge over the river was covered by an avalanche of boulders that were then cemented together by sulphur from the springs. The ice melted, and the 'bridge' remained.

A hotel was built in 1917, specifically for clients to take the hot springs, with a tunnel connecting the hotel to the baths under the bridge. The hotel thrived until 1965 when it was destroyed by an enormous avalanche.

The baths, although now disused, can still provide a refreshing hot shower.

Of the places to stay in Puente del Inca, the army hostel is worth considering. Over the entrance door to the army barracks (*Ejercito Argentina*) is a sign welcoming all mountaineers. The dedicated visitors' hostel, suitable for both sexes, can accommodate 76 visitors in bunk-bedded rooms with separate bathrooms. The bedrooms are rather basic, but the ground floor reception rooms are spacious and comfortable, and the food is good. This is the cheapest accommodation for Aconcagua.

The natural bridge over the Las Cuevas river at Puente del Inca

ROUTES TO THE SUMMIT

The Normal route

The *ruta Normal* begins about 5km west of Puente del Inca, or 10km from Los Penitentes. At the start of the route there is a gravel car park near a ranger station, with a helicopter permanently parked nearby. This is used to take medical and emergency supplies to the various basecamps and to airlift sick or injured climbers out. It is in constant use, generally landing at both basecamps at least once every day. Since its introduction in the 1999/2000 season the number of fatalities on the mountain has dropped from seven to ten per annum, to one or two.

The ranger will check the permits and issue refuse sacks. The non-return of a refuse sack carries a hefty fine. Guides may sometimes want to take charge of your refuse sack.

There is a dirt track road in for a few kilometres, but its use for vehicles is closed except in emergencies.

The start of the Normal route at the Horcones road head

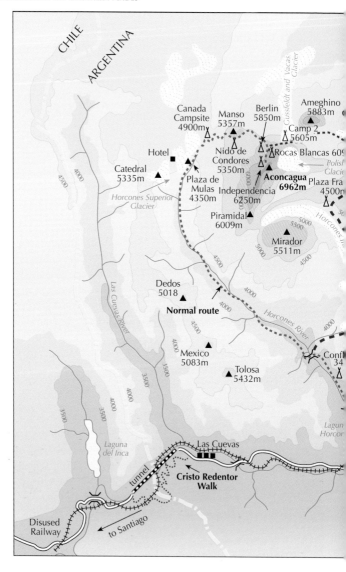

CHILE

ARGENTINA

Gussfeldt and Vacas Glacier

Canada
Campsite
4900m

Manso
5357m

Berlin
5850m

Ameghino
5883m

Camp 2
5605m

Hotel

Nido de
Condores
5350m

Rocas Blancas 609

Catedral
5335m

Plaza de
Mulas
4350m

Polish Glacie

**Aconcagua
6962m**

Plaza Fra
4500n

Independencia
6250m

*Horcones Superior
Glacier*

Piramidal
6009m

Horcones In

5000

5500

Mirador
5511m

5000

4500

Dedos
5018

Normal route

4000

Horcones River

4000

Mexico
5083m

4500

Tolosa
5432m

Confl
34

*Lagun
Horcor*

*Laguna
del Inca*

Las Cuevas

**Cristo Redentor
Walk**

tunnel

*Disused
Railway*

to Santiago

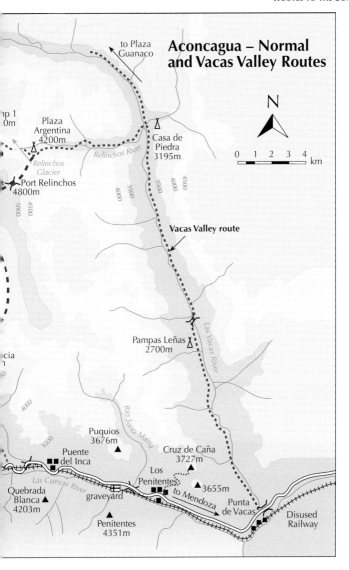

to Plaza
Guanaco

Aconcagua – Normal and Vacas Valley Routes

N

0 1 2 3 4 km

p 1
0m

Plaza
Argentina
4200m

Casa de
Piedra
3195m

Relinchos River

*Relinchos
Glacier*

Port Relinchos
4800m

Vacas Valley route

Las Vacas River

Pampas Leñas
2700m

cia

Rio Santa Maria

Puquios
3676m ▲

Cruz de Caña
3727m ▲

Puente
del Inca

Los
Penitentes

Las Cuevas River

Quebrada
Blanca ▲
4203m

graveyard

to Mendoza

▲ 3655m

Punta
de Vacas

Disused
Railway

Penitentes
4351m

The name 'Confluencia' comes from the confluence of the two rivers, that from the Horcones valley and that from the Horcones Inferior Glacier in the valley above.

About 2.5km in is the **lagoon**, where undoubtedly you will want to take more photographs. The road is stony and flat as far as the first footbridge – a gentle introduction to the ruta Normal. This steel suspension bridge was erected some years ago over the raging torrent below. After the footbridge the path initially follows the river on its eastern bank, then leaves it to rise steeply through a grey limestone boulder field before easing out to a gentle gradient on the approach to **Confluencia**. ◀

For these first two days of the journey to basecamp you will have to carry everything you need during the day and for the night in Confluencia: sleeping bag, mattress and warm clothing will be essential. The mules will have gone ahead direct to Plaza de Mulas with the main loads.

The Confluencia campsite was moved in 2007, for the second time in eight years. It is now nearly a kilometre nearer to the Horcones road head and further from Plaza de Mulas. So it is only a short 2 to 2½ hr walk from Horcones. It is now customary for trekkers to have their lunch at Los Penitentes before starting the walk.

At 3440m the **Confluencia campsite** is an open area, quite windy and very dusty. There is water available, but it generally contains a lot of magnesium, and is not pleasant to drink. It is advisable to take your own water.

The choice of location for the new campsite, understandably, is a bone of contention between the tour operators and arrieros on one side, and the park rangers on the other. Some will rest here for a day. Some will trek up to Plaza Francia and return. Those on their way out may only pause to take on water.

From the road head to Confluencia the altitude will have increased from 2580m to 3440m. It will be hot during the day at Confluencia, as high as 27ºC, falling when the sun goes down to perhaps only 6ºC at night.

Crossing the Horcones river at a shallow point

From Confluencia to Plaza de Mulas takes 7–8hrs. Initially the path runs over the river floodplain, a flat walk over gravel. You will have to cross the river three times, and if the river is full the water will cover your boots. Some will take off their boots and wade through the ice-cold water, others will run and jump, and the more practical will keep their boots on, using their walking poles to limit the damage, and wring out their socks to dry at midday.

Near to basecamp the trail becomes dramatically steeper. **Plaza de Mulas** is at an elevation of 4250m, and the last few kilometres account for most of the rise.

At the height of the season expect to find upwards of 150 tents and 50 mess tents, so that the population could be several hundred people. **Plaza de Mulas** is a relatively sheltered campsite, with good, fresh water.

71

There are a number of places to eat and drink at basecamp, with burgers, steak sandwiches and beer very popular. Hygiene is not a strong point in these make-shift cafés, however, and there have been incidences of diarrhoea.

On arrival at basecamp it is advisable to get an early indication of your saturated oxygen level. The service is free and encouraged, and the doctor's hut is in the middle of the camp. Virtually everyone takes at least one day's rest at Plaza de Mulas, some two or more days, depending on the saturated oxygen count.

A short walk to the west from basecamp is the **Hotel Plaza de Mulas**, where you can telephone the outside world, have a meal and take a shower. En route to the hotel you will encounter your first field of penitentes. The walk over to the hotel takes 20mins, over undulating ground. For the unacclimatised newcomer it will be an energy-sapping experience.

SURVIVAL TIP

At the hotel there is great demand for the two telephones in the front hall, which take only Argentinean peso coins. Most tour operators have satellite mobile phones for client use, but charges are considerably more expensive than the hotel's landline. There are internet facilities at Plaza de Mulas, but they are also quite expensive.

Above Plaza de Mulas there are three intermediate camps before the summit:
- **Camp Canada** (4900m)
- **Nido de Condores** (5350m), and finally
- **Berlin** (5850m)

It is a 3hr trek up to Canada and a further 3hrs to Nido. The Berlin camp is a 4hr trek above Nido.

The camps at Canada and Nido de Condores are ill defined, with tents pitched in no particular pattern. At Canada the campsite is south of the route up the mountain, and at Nido the route is through the campsite. At Berlin the camp is on a shoulder of the mountain,

and the tents are tightly grouped around a number of wooden huts.

Nido de Condores was elevated in 2002 to somewhat the same status as the basecamps, and now has a park ranger resident. This reflects the numbers who camp there. Some may bypass Camp Canada, and some may make their summit bid direct from Nido, but few bypass Nido.

The ranger here has significant authority. He is required to check on the condition of climbers, and may call at your tent. He can order climbers to descend if he suspects a poor medical or physical condition, or if his check establishes that a climber does not have the proper gear for this altitude.

Whereas the trail into Plaza de Mulas is generally relatively flat, except for the last few kilometres, the terrain changes significantly above the basecamp. Out over

The route out of Plaza de Mulas towards Camp Canada

SURVIVAL TIP

None of the upper camps have fresh water, so snow must be gathered for melting. Behind most boulders there are the inevitable excrement deposits (particularly at Berlin), so finding fresh clean snow may require a climb.

The route between Camp Canada and Nido de Condores

the field of penitentes from Plaza de Mulas the route is quite steep and only eases upon reaching **Camp Canada**. Halfway between Plaza de Mulas and Canada there is a rocky, isolated area known as The Conway Stones, named after a 19th-century English scientist and mountaineer. Just after leaving Camp Canada you will pass a giant stone known as the 5000m Stone.

As the altitude increases the night-time temperature and wind chill become more significant. At basecamp there can be a considerable degree of movement around the camp at night. There will be discussions and the occasional singsong. At the upper camps the cold will drive all into their sleeping bags as soon as the sun sets, and few will venture out until the sun shines on the tent again in the morning.

Up to **Nido de Condores** the emphasis will be on steady trekking, acclimatisation, taking things easy, regular resting, carrying a load up to return and sleep at a lower camp. After Nido that pattern changes. Upon reaching **Berlin** the focus is on the summit. Spending a rest day at an altitude of 5850m is not to be recommended. The air is thin, it is difficult to sleep, appetites are poor and the weather can be treacherous. The best plan is to make ready at Berlin and set off early the next morning for the summit.

In the late afternoon at Berlin climbers will be returning from their summit attempt. Those who have made it will be in high spirits and may continue their celebrations into the night, much to the annoyance of those who are trying to gain a degree of peaceful repose (sleep might be too much to hope for) before their early morning venture. There will be drama too as anxious eyes watch the skyline at dusk for comrades who are on their way down. There will be the occasional scramble from the camp to help exhausted climbers make it back.

The sunsets at Berlin can be spectacular, and well worth staying up for. As every mountain climber knows, the sky at night over such places can be so clear, the stars so vivid.

Berlin camp

Trekking through the Vacas Valley

The Vacas Valley route

The Vacas Valley route starts at Punta de Vacas, 7km east of Los Penitentes. Activity at the road head is much quieter than further west at the start of the Normal route. There is no ranger, no helicopter and no mule station. A ruined stone hut is the only distinguishing landmark.

Steeper and more rugged than the Normal route, the trail rises and falls with the river, winding over steep scree. There is good shelter from the sun and wind, however. You will be aware immediately of the solitude, interrupted by scurrying lizards and singing birds.

AN ENCOUNTER AT PAMPA DE LEÑAS

Two Londoners were resting at Pampa de Leñas, en route from Plaza Argentina to Punta de Vacas. They were originally three, but one had to be airlifted out due to altitude sickness. The two had reached Camp 2 and were preparing for a summit attempt. It was extremely cold in the early morning, the temperature at -15°C. One of them had removed his gloves in order to put on and tie his boots. When he put the gloves back on he could not get the circulation back into all his fingers. Nevertheless he started the climb. After an hour he stopped and discussed his problem with the guide. Vain attempts were made to warm his hands, but it was not possible to get the blood in his thumbs to circulate. Eventually he returned to camp, and his comrade proceeded to the summit. Warm water failed to relieve the problem. At basecamp the doctor had bandaged the thumbs, but was doubtful that they could be saved. They were now turning black.

The friends further related how they had been in the company of a Korean on the inward journey from Punta de Vacas. At Pampa de Leñas the Korean had decided to flex his muscles by climbing the cliff above the camp. He had fallen and was seriously injured. They were now informed that the Korean died on the way to hospital.

The initial journey ends at **Pampa de Leñas** after 4–5hrs. Expect the day to be arduous and hot. You will know that you are within 15 mins of the campsite when you have to cross a fast-flowing stream that has clean drinking water.

Pampa de Leñas is at an elevation of 2800m, so the height gained on the first day is very small. There will only be a few tents at this campsite, where the ranger and his family live. The area is nestled under high cliffs, sheltered and peaceful. Potable water is available from a tap near the ranger station.

The trail the second day to Casa de Piedra is very similar, once again with very little elevation achieved. On the journey you will cross a footbridge 1km north of Pampa de Leñas and later see cattle grazing on the river's edge.

The footbridge over the Vacas river outside Pampa de Leñas

The Pampa de Leñas campsite

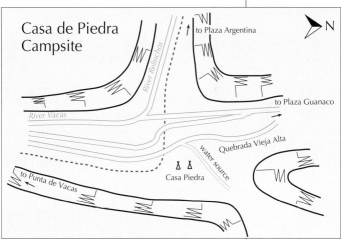

Casa de Piedra Campsite

River Relinchos

to Plaza Argentina

to Plaza Guanaco

River Vacas

Quebrada Vieja Alta

water source

Casa Piedra

to Punta de Vacas

N

On arrival at **Casa de Piedra** there is a wonderful view of Aconcagua from the Polish Glacier side. As you approach the campsite clearing, Cerro Ameghino initially comes into view, followed soon by the awesome bulk of Aconcagua.

Casa de Piedra, at an elevation of 3195m, is a disjointed campsite alongside the river. There is a rough stone structure – from which the site gets its name – built into an enormous isolated conglomerate rock on the eastern bank. In and around this stone structure the arrieros will camp. In the past, climbers could cross the river immediately and camp, so that boots and socks could be dried out by morning, but this is no longer permitted.

The river at Casa de Piedra has many tributaries, so there are multiple crossing points. If you decide to arrange for a mule to carry you across the river in the morning, bear in mind that you will nevertheless get wet further up the valley towards Plaza Argentina. So, it is perhaps better to face up to wearing your sandals and carrying your boots, and getting wet like everyone else.

From Casa de Piedra up the **Relinchos Valley** the trail is tough. ◄ There are many climbs around the steep valley sides, and a few river crossings. One crossing must be made approximately a third of the way up, where the river is deep and fast flowing. The water is ice cold and the riverbed stony.

Plaza Argentina at 4200m is at a slightly lower elevation than Plaza de Mulas. It is 5–6hrs walk from Casa de Piedra up through the Relinchos Valley. ◄ The Relinchos

This is the most likely stretch to see guanacos, possibly dead ones. They are fragile and prone to falling on rocky terrain.

A little over halfway up the valley you can rest and have lunch in a boulder field on the side of the trail.

Crossing the river at Casa Piedra

Glacier hangs above the campsite and dictates much of the trail above it. Similar to the Lower Horcones Glacier it is covered in scree, eventually giving way to flat land that leads into **Plaza Argentina**. The camp lies on undulating glacial moraine, so that many of the tents may be hidden from view.

> **Plaza Argentina** has the same facilities, on a smaller scale, as Plaza de Mulas, and at the height of the season there may be up to 50 tents and 15 mess tents. The doctor and the ranger will be here, but there is no hotel and no phone link to the outside world.

Above Plaza Argentina there are three intermediate camps before the summit (attempts at assigning names to the lower camps have so far failed):
- **Camp 1** (4850m)
- **Camp 2** (5605m), and finally
- **Rocas Blancas** (6095m).

The climb from basecamp to Camp 1 is a gruelling 5hrs through fields of penitentes, and over a glacier with rough scree deposits. Often you have the choice of scrambling over loose gravelly moraine or negotiating a way through the penitentes. The eventual approach into **Camp 1** is a left-hand turn over deep snow and ice, entering the camp over a boulder field.

> **Camp 1** is a linear campsite is on a windy shoulder on the mountain, with the tents protected by walls of stones. Water is available from the icy river that flows alongside.

From Camp 1 to Camp 2 the elevation increases by over 750m, again a tough day's climb taking 5–6hrs. There is a col midway that makes a good resting point. This col is often used as an intermediate campsite, commonly referred to as 'Camp 1½'. It has an expansive flat open area.

A windswept Camp 2 at 5600m

Camp 2, like Nido de Condores, is the most popular site above Plaza Argentina to rest. It is an open camp with little protection from the wind and sun. Fresh water flows through the icy river beside the camp.

Above the campsite, under a cliff face, there is the grave of an Argentinean who died in 1983. The grave is rather shallow and portions of his clothes and body are exposed.

From Camp 2 to Rocas Blancas it is a mere 3hrs of easy climbing, occasionally over ice. The route is around the rear of the mountain. Crampons and an ice axe will be essential to negotiate the short ice field.

Many dispense with the last camp, preferring to sleep better at Camp 2 and make the summit attempt from there. However, a climb on summit day of 1355m, or double the previous days' climbs, is extremely demanding. Going for the summit from Camp 2 means you have to stop and don your crampons at the ice field, then take them off beyond it. This loses precious time on the most important day.

Rocas Blancas, also referred to as Piedras Blancas (small as opposed to large rocks), is an exposed site nestled against the white rocks from which it takes its name. There is no water.

Summit day

To reach Berlin or Rocas Blancas is half the work of climbing Aconcagua. The second and most crucial part is summit day. You must now concentrate all your energies for that last push.

Rocas Blancas is just off the Normal route above Camp Berlin. From Berlin there is an initial steep scramble to reach the stony path. From Rocas Blancas the trail to rejoin the Normal route is good and easy. Where the trails meet the climb is steady to a col where there is a ruined wooden hut known as **Independencia** (6380m). ▶ Some climbers may opt to camp here and shorten summit day by a further hour or so.

Independencia is a popular spot for a rest and a drink, perhaps also a convenient place to don crampons, depending on the weather.

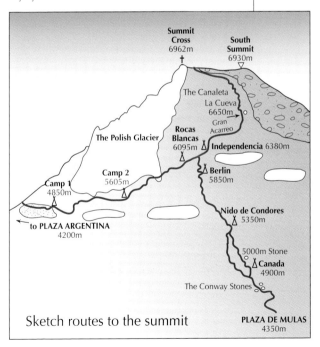

Sketch routes to the summit

The climb from Independencia is steady and traverses up to a ridge known as Cresta del Viento. Here you turn left to cross a very exposed area where the wind is unrelenting. Beyond the Cresta del Viento is the Gran Acarreo, a traverse that leads to the base of **The Canaleta** (6660m). The **Gran Acarreo** is relatively easy, but the terrain becomes loose underfoot.

To classify The Canaleta as a slagheap is perhaps disingenuous, but most apt. The mixture of loose sand and gravel is frustrating, for with every two steps taken you slide back one. The Canaleta is 400m high and takes several hours to ascend. Occasionally it is covered in frozen snow, making it relatively easy to climb in crampons. Near its base is a shelter under a cliff face, known as **La Cueva**, where climbers leave rucksacks, taking only the bare essentials to the summit. Here guides will encourage climbers to summon up all their remaining strength for this final assault.

At the top of The Canaleta there is a gentle traverse to negotiate and some large boulders to overcome before arriving at the summit. Above this gentle traverse the ridge is known as the Cresta del Guanaco. It connects the **south summit** to the north summit. On the north summit (6960m), the highest point of the Americas is marked by a simple aluminium cross.

On a clear day views from the summit can be stunning. To the southwest you can see Tupungato mountain. Below is the south face with the Horcones Inferior Glacier and Plaza Francia visible.

Almost every climber brings a memento to the summit – scarves, bandanas, flags, and so on – so that by the end of the season the tiny cross can hardly be seen. The ice and snow of the winter, however, is a natural clearer, and by spring, the cross is restored to its isolation.

Wind chill and the cold

For every 100m of altitude gained there will be a drop of between half and one degree in the temperature. So if it is -5°C at basecamp you can expect it to be -25°C approaching the summit. Remember also that the higher the wind speed the greater the wind chill. (See the table overleaf.)

Exposure of bare flesh to a wind chill of more than -20°C for anything but a few seconds will lead to problems, and exposure of the flesh to a wind chill of -30°C

View from the summit towards the south. Note climbers on the ridge at the bottom left of the picture..

85

WIND CHILL CALCULATOR				
No wind	20km/h	30km/h	40km/h	60km/h
0°C	-10°C	-12°C	-16°C	-20°C
-10°C	-23°C	-26°C	-33°C	-36°C
-20°C	-33°C	-40°C	-50°C	-55°C
-30°C	-47°C	-55°C	-62°C	-70°C

at all will lead to frostbite. At high wind chill levels your balaclava should completely cover your face.

You must keep your fingers and toes moving as much as possible. Stretch them as often as you can. Getting them out of the wind will help enormously. If you feel that you may have been over exposed then try to get some hot liquid inside you, preferably with lots of sugar. Movement will bring a heat flow into the body, although it will use up your store of energy.

Those eight hand warmers that were recommended (see 'Preparations') – four of them were intended for use on summit day, one in each glove early in the morning, refreshed mid morning, while the remaining four were intended for emergencies. If you can get a hand warmer to an affected area it could be the difference between losing and saving a finger or toe.

In the event of a storm
The golden rule is to stick to whoever you are with. The most likely time for snow to fall is in the afternoon, when people are descending. A complete white out can leave a climber most exposed, so try to team up with others, rope up, and share your decisions.

Getting down safely
Aconcagua is not unlike other high mountains where fatalities are generally more likely to occur on the descent rather than the ascent. The sense of euphoria at reaching the summit may tend to block out the reality that beckons. The mind and body will be tired. To compound the

risk, the mountain is more prone to poor weather in the afternoon.

Roping up on The Canaleta should be mandatory, as this is the most dangerous part of the descent. On the approach to Berlin there is another dangerous section where a rock outcrop must be negotiated.

THE JANUARY 2009 DEATHS

In early 2009 there were four deaths on the mountain in three separate incidents within a few days of each other.

The first to die was an architect from Cologne in Germany. He had been climbing on the Polish Glacier with a Canadian he had met at Plaza Argentina. They had set off for the summit together, but later split, with the Canadian pushing on for the summit while his companion decided to descend. The weather was poor and conditions under foot on the glacier far from ideal, with a soft snow capping in places.

Eventually the weather forced the Canadian to retreat, but as he descended he noticed an object on the rocks far below him, which turned out to be the architect's body.

On the same day four Italians – two men and two women – and their Mendocino guide, an accomplished mountaineer living in the United States, made it with difficulty to the summit. The weather set in and the five became separated. None returned to camp that night. The next day, during a break in the weather, they were spotted, but again, no one returned to camp. Miraculously, two days after reaching the summit three of the Italians were rescued, although they all suffered severe frostbite to fingers and hands. Sadly one of the women and the guide died.

On the same day that the Italians were rescued a 42 year old Englishman died of a heart attack after successfully reaching the summit.

It was unusual for four people to die on the mountain within a few days, and it sent shockwaves through the local community. The Mendoza press gave extensive coverage to the the story and senior climbers were interviewed at length. The consensus was that the climbers, other than the last one, should not have been where they were. The two on the Polish Glacier should have known that conditions underfoot were treacherous, and the glacier was unsafe to be on that day. The Italians and their guide should have returned to Camp Berlin when they saw the weather was closing in.

SUMMARY COMPARISON OF NORMAL & VACAS VALLEY ROUTES

	Normal Route	Vacas Valley Route
Distance to basecamp	36km	47km
Distance to summit	Shorter	Longer, because of traverse around to the Normal route
Difficulty	Easier	Harder to basecamp/Camp 2
	Shallow rivers	Deeper rivers
Time	Shorter	At least two days longer
Water	None above basecamp	Streams up to Camp 2
Wildlife	Relatively barren	Greener, more visible
Interest	Lots of people	Fewer people, more interesting countryside
Statistical probability of reaching the summit	Lower	Higher
Cost	Lower	Two day's extra cost

The long walk out

Most trekkers will take a day to descend from Berlin to Plaza de Mulas. Similarly, a day is the usual time from Rocas Blancas to Plaza Argentina. On the Vacas Valley route the descent is much slower than the Normal route. The fields of penitentes make trekking slow, and many will reach basecamp late in the day.

Although the climbing is over, and the air is becoming thicker, the day is a difficult one. All the gear that was taken up in loads on previous days must now be taken down in one go. Those arriving at the top camps will be pleasantly surprised to be offered excess food and fuel oil. Guides will bundle food and fuel and leave it for future visits.

On the track down stumbling and falling will be inevitable, and here the trekking poles provide good balance. The monotony will be broken by sudden surges as trekkers throw caution to the wind and virtually ski down the steeper gravelly paths. Rucksack straps should be pulled tight into the chest to avoid back strain.

The beer at basecamp that was forbidden a week before, that was so expensive a week before, is drunk in

The descent to Plaza de Mulas

copious amounts by descenders. The walk to the hotel next morning to make that phone call home now takes only a few minutes.

It is a long arduous day from Plaza de Mulas to the road head. Trekkers will look in envy at the arrieros on their horses. The care that was taken over the rivers on the way up will be ignored as the returning trekkers plunge regardless into the water. At Confluencia, where a well-earned rest is inevitable, it will be difficult to motivate the limbs to rise up and make that final effort to the road. On the Vacas Valley

Fast food at Plaza de Mulas

route it is customary to make an overnight stop at Casa de Piedra, but many continue the 42km to Punta de Vacas.

OTHER ROUTES
Vacas Valley ascent, Normal route descent

The best of both worlds is to ascend via the Vacas Valley route and descend via the Normal route. This provides the time and difficulty on the Vacas Valley route to acclimatise yet shortens the overall trip by a day. It also allows you to see and compare the two routes.

The difficulty with changing the ascent and descent is that the gear left at basecamp Plaza Argentina must be sent out to the road head and returned to Plaza de Mulas. However, if this arrangement is in place with the guide or mule company before the start there should be no difficulty. Mules are making the trips in and out and across every day. The other essential ingredient in changing over is that top camp must be at Rocas Blancas; otherwise it would be necessary to traverse over and back to Camp 2 to collect the tent and other gear.

Confluencia to Plaza Argentina

There is a route from Confluencia via Plaza Francia to Plaza Argentina. This involves climbing up to 5100m over Port Relinchos, also known as the Ibañez col, before descending into Plaza Argentina. This route is only possible when the level of snow at Port Relinchos is comparatively low, so would require some advance information. It is a difficult ascent, but a most dangerous descent, so that a route out from Plaza Argentina to Confluencia is not an option.

Since a porter died descending the col into Plaza Francia the rangers have now closed the route.

The Polish Glacier direct traverse

From Camp 2 on the Vacas Valley route there is a direct ascent to the summit of Aconcagua via the Polish Glacier,

*Arrieros return down
the Horcones Valley
after a hard day*

avoiding the Canaleta. The glacier is notoriously unstable
and unpredictable, and gaining good grips with crampons
and ice axes can be difficult. Nevertheless, the route is
direct and consequently much shorter.

From the summit it is possible to ski or snowboard
down the Polish Glacier to Camp 2.

Vacas Valley via Plaza Guanaco

There is another route via the Vacas Valley. Instead of turning at Casa Piedra the route continues up, following the
Vacas river, through Quebrada Vieja Alta (high old valley).

A kilometre out of Casa Piedra there is a significant
stream to cross, and then there is a long, flat walk bend-
ing to the west. The river must be crossed again further
up the valley. Passing a disused refugio at 3435m you
eventually arrive at an open area which is Plaza Guanaco
(4000m). From basecamp three intermediate camps will
be necessary before the route meets the others above
Independencia.

The Plaza Guanaco route is currently closed to protect the wildlife (guanaco). It is much longer than the
other routes, there is little gain in height in the long valley, and there is no rescue service. The only advantage
would be that there would be fewer people.

PART 2
ACONCAGUA, VALLECITOS AND THE
MAIPO VOLCANO

The Tolosa mountain viewed from Cristo Redentor

ROUTES NEAR ACONCAGUA

The best approach is to get used to the altitude gradually, so before heading off on a major expedition check out the local scene. In and around Puente del Inca and Los Penitentes there are gentle, flat walks, and a few arduous ones to follow on with and help you acclimatise.

Andinistas Graveyard

Along the road between Puente del Inca and Los Penitentes there is a graveyard to those who have died in this part of the Andes. The graveyard is immediately beside the road, 2.5km from Los Penitentes and 3.5km from Puente del Inca. It is a sombre place, with many plaques of relatively recent origin.

Natural History Museum

About 2km along the road from Los Penitentes east towards Punta de Vacas there is a former railway structure that has been converted into a small makeshift museum. This is a fun place, not to be taken too seriously. The owner has used his skills to erect pumps and pulleys to show how volcanoes work. He has rock and mineral samples, and his paintings display the history of the Andes. An illustrated lecture tour (in Spanish, but most will get a good grasp) costs a few pesos.

There is an option of continuing the walk along the road towards Punta de Vacas. At a bend in the road, a few kilometres further on, there is a clear view through the valleys to Tupungato (6550m).

Trekking paths above Los Penitentes

93

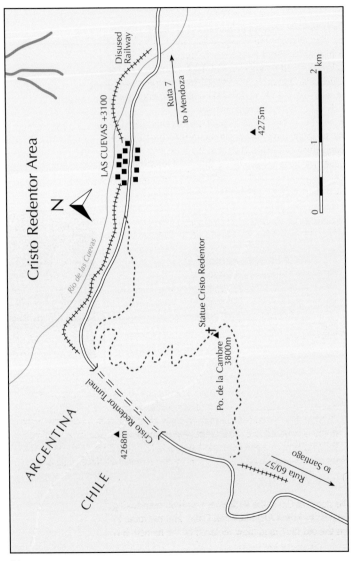

Cristo Redentor Area

Trekking paths above Los Penitentes

There are treks up the mountain at Los Penitentes, following the cable car and skiing routes. These will take you as high as 3727m, which is Cerro Cruz de Caña. Simply follow the well defined ski path up and into the ravine (Quebrada Cruz de Caña), from where the mountain will be seen ahead. Treks up these ski slopes are very popular with those staying in Los Penitentes.

Out of Puente del Inca on the south side there is a trek up to the top of Banderita (Cerro Blanca on the new map) which is 4203m. The route is via the first valley to the left on the road towards Las Cuevas. It is a tough day-long trek. There is the further choice of Cerro Blanca to the west, even higher at 4411m.

A walk to the statue of Cristo Redentor

Time	Half day
Distance	8km round trip
Terrain	Dirt road
Maximum elevation	3800m
Total climb	700m
Water source	No

This is a stiff walk intended as an introduction to the altitude. In the summer months, between January and March, the walk will be over dry ground. Outside these periods there may be snow lying. The area around the great statue is exposed and windswept, and warm gear is essential at all times. Trekking boots are recommended, particularly for the descent. If you are not yet acclimatised, expect to take 3hrs for the ascent, and 1hr coming down.

The statue of Christ the Redeemer was built overlooking the pass between Argentina and Chile, and the route to it is the old RN7 road (now replaced by the tunnel). It is accessible with a four-wheel drive vehicle in dry weather, but the route is tough and difficult, and deteriorates further every year.

To get to the old road you have to make for the village of **Las Cuevas** (3100m), 12km from Puente del Inca. The old road leads off to the south of the village under an arched building. Multiple hairpin bends wind up the hillside. ◄

You wonder how cars and trucks coped with the climb in the not-too-distant past.

The trek is most rewarding, however, as the col is a very interesting, ghostly place. An old stone building on one side welcomes travellers to Argentina, while close by is another that is clearly Chilean. The enormous statue has many plaques, the principal one signifying its importance as a symbol of peace between the two countries.

Across the valley is the imposing mountain of Tolosa with its high hanging glacier in the shape of a man with no legs – *el hombre coja*.

The easiest route down is along the steep spine that cuts through the road.

Horcones Valley to Plaza Francia

Time	3–4 day trek
Distance	65km round trip
Terrain	Varied terrain
Maximum elevation	5000m
Total climb	2420m
Water sources	No

This trek is in towards the south face of Aconcagua and leads up to a relatively high elevation. It is not difficult and the effort required is well worth the elevation gained and you will be rewarded with excellent views.

Plaza Francia is an ill-defined camp near the south face. It is not necessary to travel all the way in to the Plaza Francia to experience the wonderful vista of the south

face and the Horcones Inferior Glacier; a stop at 4000m will achieve this. However, between 4000m and 5000m is an easy walk over good ground. At this altitude there are many suitable places to camp. Thus, the trekker can vary the distance travelled up the valley to suit his composure and condition.

The Horcones Inferior Glacier is up to 20m thick in places

The route follows the ruta Normal from the Horcones ranger station, past the Horcones Lagoon and up to Camp Confluencia. The first day of the trek is easy, and the 15km point will be reached in about 2–3hrs. From Confluencia the trail gets tougher, rising out of the relatively flat Horcones Valley, in and up to the right, around boulders and over rough, steep ground. After about 2hrs the valley widens and the trail is an even gradient over good ground, climbing from 3500m to 4500m.

There are campsites 6km from Confluencia, not very far from clean water. In the main valley there are ample sheltered sites to pitch a tent. However, up in the valley there is no clean water. Sources of clean water near the south face are also difficult to locate, depending on the melted water from the face itself.

It would be best to spend the first night at Confluencia, the second at Plaza Francia or an intermediate site, and the third back at Confluencia. Alternatively, it is possible to trek from Confluencia up and back in one day.

Plaza Francia is normally deserted, as relatively few climbers attempt the south face. A ruined hut marks the original campsite. At Plaza Francia the enormity of Aconcagua can be experienced. The 3000m-high by 7000m-wide wall of rock, snow and ice is a daunting spectacle. With binoculars you can look up to the summit. If there are climbers on the face, watching them can be interesting.

On the left the great Horcones Inferior Glacier creaks and groans as this living mass works its way down the valley.

Detail of the hanging glaciers on Aconcagua's south face

ROUTES FROM VALLECITOS

VALLECITOS SKI AND MOUNTAIN LODGE

Vallecitos (pronounced baay-ay-see-tos) is a convenient, practical and inexpensive centre to acclimatise for Aconcagua. This small privately owned ski resort is dedicated, during the summer months, to acclimatisation. The proprietor, Alejandro Geras, is himself a high mountain climber and guide.

Vallecitos is 1½hrs drive from Mendoza, on the road towards Aconcagua. The centre operates transport from Mendoza and to Aconcagua. It should be emphasised that the mountain lodge is small, generally only able to cater for 40 people, and the facilities are very basic.

Vallecitos (2980m) can act as a camp for one-day or half-day treks, or as a basecamp for two to four day treks. From the centre there are short treks to 4000m and above, and longer treks to 5700m and even up to 6300m. Guided treks and mule services are available. Alternatively there is a campsite above the centre, with fresh water and many choices of unguided treks.

The steep road to Vallecitos is off the Ruta 7, less than an hour from Mendoza towards Aconcagua. At Potrerillos a paved road to the left leads towards La Chacrita, then forks right to rise on a dirt track to Vallecitos.

The Vallecitos ski centre

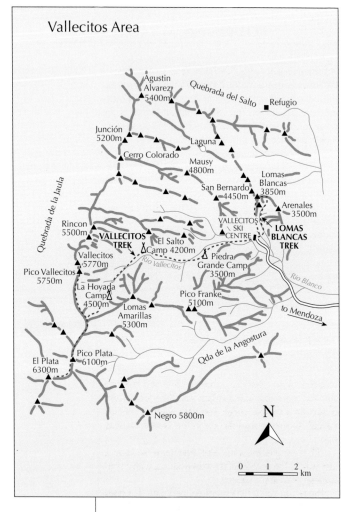

Vallecitos Area

Agustin
Alvarez
5400m

Quebrada del Salto

Refugio

Junción
5200m

Laguna

Cerro Colorado

Mausy
4800m

Lomas
Blancas
3850m

San Bernardo
4450m

Arenales
3500m

VALLECITOS
SKI
CENTRE

LOMAS
BLANCAS
TREK

Rincon
5500m

VALLECITOS
TREK

El Salto
Camp 4200m

Quebrada de la Jaula

Vallecitos
5770m

Río Vallecitos

Piedra
Grande Camp
3500m

Río Blanco

Pico Vallecitos
5750m

La Hoyada
Camp
4500m

Pico Franke
5100m

to Mendoza

Lomas
Amarillas
5300m

El Plata
6300m

Pico Plata
6100m

Qda de la Angostura

Negro 5800m

N

0   1   2
km

The small ski centre is a motley collection of huts, all
shut during the summer except for the lodge. Bedrooms
have bunk beds with four separate bathrooms. There is

hot water, a public telephone and barbecue facilities. At night a fire blazes in the dining room. There are no frills here – food is simple and basic, no carpets, central heating or television.

The campsite above the resort is at an elevation of 3200m on a flat area of open ground known as Las Vegas (the springs). Vallecitos is a popular area for hill walkers and climbers at weekends. If you intend to stay at the lodge, and/or to go on guided treks, it is advisable to book in advance.

Lomas Blancas 3850m

Time	Half day
Distance	9km round trip
Terrain	Easy
Maximum elevation	3850m
Total climb	950m
Water sources	No

This is an easy introductory climb.

From the lodge cross the entrance road and take the route that goes east into a valley, and then turns north up through a narrow gorge. The path winds it way up to a col. To the west of the col is the **Lomas Blancas** peak.

There are guanacos in these mountains, so keep a close watch. The peak itself is a rocky hilltop, with a simple metal cross at the summit.

The return can be via an ill-defined path that goes south from the summit over rock outcrops, eventually coming down over relatively steep ground onto the ski runs.

Cerro Vallecitos 5770m

Time	4-day trek
Distance	37km round trip
Terrain	Moderate
Maximum elevation	5770m
Total climb	2870
Water sources	No

This trek can be varied to suit the weather and the physical condition of the participants. The trek is up towards the snow-capped peaks where there are choices of how far to go and which peak to climb.

The most popular choices, on non-technical routes are:
* Cerro Vallecitos (5770m)
* Pico Plata (6100m)
* El Plata (6300m), beyond Pico Plata.

The route is simple, and it would be difficult to go astray. From the rear of the lodge ascend to the northeast, up over the crest, following the river.

There are four campsites above the Vallecitos centre. The first is at Las Vegas on a flat grassy site (3200m). The second is at **Piedra Grande** (3500m), a short walk further into the valley. **El Salto** (the Jump, 4000m) is 3–4hrs beyond Piedra Grande, via a narrow ravine and up over moraine. It is possible to trek from the centre to El Salto, with a full pack, in one day. At El Salto water depends on the degree of melting snow above, but generally the stream – **Río Vallecitos** – is adequate.

Top camp is **La Hoyada** (The Pot, 4500m), 4hrs above El Salto. The route follows the stream as it bends up to the southwest. The campsite is sheltered inside an inverted cone-shaped area. Once again water is not too far away and is dependent on melted ice and snow from above.

Summit day to Cerro Vallecitos is arduous. The climb of over 1200m is a long day that should start before 4am. The route is up to the col, then a turn to the right and north. The first peak is **Pico Vallecitos** (5750m). Beyond it over to the north is **Cerro Vallecitos** (5770m).

The Cerro Vallecitos summit is an exposed area of solid rock

From La Hoyada the route to **Pico Plata** (6100m) and **El Plata** (6300m) is in the same initial direction, except that, upon ascending the ridge, you turn south and left. The trek is much steeper and longer than the trek to Vallecitos.

You can comfortably get back from La Hoyada to the hostel in one day.

The hostel can arrange to deliver a mule load to El Salto. This makes the first day's trek less onerous. Some provisions can be stored at El Salto, so that only the minimum is taken to La Hoyada.

The Maipo Volcano with guanacos in the foreground

THE MAIPO VOLCANO

150km south of Mendoza there is an old pass between Chile and Argentina beside the Maipo Volcano. Under the volcano there is a lake, Laguna Diamante, renowned for its brown trout. If you go there you are guaranteed to come back with a camera full of pictures of gu6anacos.

To get to the Maipo Volcano requires a four wheel drive vehicle, or certainly a robust pick-up truck, as there are 60 kms of dirt track road to pass through. The route is directly south of Mendoza, through the town of Tunuyan, and passing the town of San Carlos. At Pareditas you leave the main road heading for San Rafael, and take the road towards the southwest. The dirt track road, due west, to Laguna Diamante is marked. It is not possible to go to the Maipo Volcano on the Chilean side, as the area is a restricted zone.

This wildlife haven is protected, and there are park rangers here. There is no admission charge, and the ranger stations have information on the flora, fauna and geology of the area.

The elevation of the lake is 3300m, while the summit of the volcano is at 5323m. The lake is believed to be a caldera where a former volcano collapsed in Quaternary times, up to five million years ago. The current volcano arose from this caldera. The approach to the lake passes interesting geological formations, some expanses of open conglomerate and some ravines with fossil-bearing sedimentary layers.

There are herds of guanacos everywhere, and they are not as timid as you may find in other parks, as here they have learned to live with the tourists.

The former pass into Chile is south of the volcano. Those who climb the volcano generally make a camp on the north side of the lake, then above this two further camps are generally made, each approximately 600m higher than the last. There are no technical difficulties en route to the summit. Inka Expediciones is one of a number of operators who include the Maipo Volcano as an optional climb.

Brown trout caught in Laguna Diamante

Tupungato Provincial Park

PART 3
TUPUNGATO AREA

TUPUNGATO

To the mountaineers of Argentina and Chile the name Tupungato evokes feelings not accorded to any other mountain. Many come to this area to climb Aconcagua – because it is high, they will say, but Tupungato epitomises more of what the Andes is all about. It is a long journey in from the road to get to Tupungato, but it is worth every step, whether it is through the wilderness of Tupungato Provincial Park or through the rugged valleys of Chile's Colorado River.

Tupungato (6550m) is a dormant volcano lying on the border between Chile and Argentina, just under 100km south of Aconcagua. It is the 12th highest mountain in the Americas. A volcanic eruption was recorded as recently as 1986, but this was on Tupungato's little sister, Tupungatito (5640m), a few kilometres to the south. There is no crater on Tupungato, but a smoking crater on Tupungatito. On the eastern face of Tupungato there is a near vertical face, some 2000m high, first climbed in 1985, but the two Argentinean climbers tragically died on the descent on the southern side.

Tupungato does not attract many climbers, and virtually none from abroad. Even with the discovery of a crashed plane in its glacier, when the mountain received world recognition, the numbers of visitors has only slightly increased. This is most certainly due in part to its remoteness.

Matthias Zurbriggen and Stuart Vines were the first to climb Tupungato in 1897. They were part of the Aconcagua expedition led by Edward Fitzgerald.

Tupungato from Portezuelo del Fraile (Friar's Col)

THE MOUNTAIN, THE GLACIER, THE AEROPLANE & THE LOST GOLD

A scheduled British South American Airways flight from Buenos Aires to Santiago mysteriously disappeared on 2 August 1947. The British Lancaster was named The Stardust and had six passengers and a crew of four.

The colourful characters among its passengers fuelled speculation over its disappearance. One was a diplomat carrying secret documents from the British king. Relations between Britain and Argentina were tense at the time, and it was considered that these documents, to be delivered to Santiago, were of particular importance. Another was a Palestinian who had a large diamond sewn into the lining of his coat. A German widow was returning to Chile with the ashes of her husband.

The plane had flown from Buenos Aires to Mendoza, and was over the Andes on the final leg of its journey. Its route was to circle around Aconcagua before landing in Santiago. The pilot radioed a message to Santiago reporting that all was well, despite a storm over the Andes, and that he expected to land in four minutes. A Morse-coded message was then received from the plane, spelling out the letters S T E N D E C. At 5.45pm the plane disappeared, never to be heard of again.

Rumours spread fast. There were reports that the plane, a converted Lancaster bomber, was carrying a cargo of gold. The widow, with her little urn, was transformed into a Nazi spy.

Over 50 years later, on 26 January 1998, two young climbers from Buenos Aires, Pablo Reguera and Fernando Garmendia, were 4500m up on Tupungato when Pablo spotted part of an engine on the ground, with the words 'OLLS-ROYCE' inscribed on it.

'How did they get a car up here?', Pablo mused. The two searched the area and found other objects, such as clothing including pieces of a heavily pinstriped suit. However, the two climbers did not realise the significance of their find. They took no photographs, and made no record of the location. After a successful summit of Tupungato the climbers descended, casually mentioning their find to the army ranger.

The ranger, Armando Cardozo, asked other climbers to watch out for wreckage, but there were no more sightings. Nine months later Armando was having lunch with a lost planes enthusiast, José Moiso, when he recalled the incident. José had been brought up near an airbase on the outskirts of Buenos Aires, and had a passion for lost planes and mountaineering. When he was a child one of his father's great stories was about the missing Lancaster, with its valuable cargo. He had already surveyed the wreckage of a Fairchild FH22 plane, which

Army ranger Armando Cardozo and mountaineer Pablo Reguera

crashed while carrying a team of rugby players. José persuaded Cardozo, himself an accomplished climber, to accompany him on an expedition. They set off in March 1999, but were caught up in a violent storm, and had to retreat without ever finding the wreckage site. A year later José and Cardozo returned in the company of José's son Alejo. They located the wreckage at 4800m. Thus began the search that resulted in a major army expedition, of 100 soldiers and as many mules trekking up the mountain, and a flood of international reporters.

Scientific investigations established the aircraft crashed due to navigational error. The pilot had radioed that he was ascending to 24,000ft to avoid a storm. In the clouds, with no landmarks to guide him (and in 1947 positioning systems were non-existent) he had calculated his course and position. He was unaware of a 300mph jet stream and thought he was on course to descend to Santiago when he crashed into Tupungato. The Lancaster hit the mountain and fell onto the glacier. A resulting avalanche covered it. The glacier apparently swallowed up the wreckage and slowly carried it down the mountain, to emerge at its base 50 years later.

The fact that neither the gold nor the diamond were ever found continues to attract those with the energy and ability to search. Some documents have emerged, but disintegrated before it could be established if they related to important Anglo-Argentinean relations. Amongst the most amazing discoveries were the aircraft wheels, fully inflated. Ninety per cent of the wreckage is still buried in the glacier, which yields up a little more of its cargo every year. No one has ever solved the mystery of the Morse-coded S T E N D E C.

SUMMARY COMPARISON OF TUPUNGATO ROUTES

	Rio Colorado	*Rio Azufre*	*Friar's Col*	*Rio Tupungato*
Basecamp	48km	50km	43km	75km
Mule trek	48km	40km	28km/35km	65km
Mule stop	Vegas del Flojo	Portezuelo Tupungato	Friar's Col	Portezuelo Tupungato
Permits	Difrol, Army, AES Gener	Army	Army	None
Difficulties	River crossing at Mal Paso	Few	Friar's Col Ascent/ descent Rio de Las Tunas crossing	Few
Water	Good sources, but irregular	Good	Clean water intermittent	Good
Total time	12 days	13 days	12/14 days	14 days

TUPUNGATO ROUTES

There are four recognised routes up Tupungato:
- via Chile, following the Rio Colorado (the most popular route)
- Two from Tupungato town in Argentina:
  – via the Rio Azufre
  – via the Portezuelo del Fraile (Friar's Col)
- the fourth from Punta de Vacas in Argentina, via the Rio Tupungato.

All the routes in Argentina go through the Tupungato Provincial Park.

The table above summarises the four routes. The distances to basecamp include how far the mules can travel. Thus, on the Rio Colorado route the mules go all the way to basecamp (in summer months only). For the routes via Argentina it is necessary to carry all gear for a further 10km approximately. On the Friar's Col route the distance the mules can trek to is determined by the ground conditions – too much snow or ice and they have to abandon after 28km, 7km short – 7km that is steep and difficult – so the total carry could be as long as 15 km.

There is a complication. There are two Rio Azufres, one on the Chilean side and the other in Argentina. On the Chilean side the Rio Azufre is a tributary of the Rio Colorado. On the Argentinean side the route follows that country's Rio Azufre, which joins the Rio de Las Tunas near the town of Tupungato.

The Tupungato River valley from Punta de Vacas

All routes entail multiple river crossings. Via the Friar's Col route there is a major crossing of the Rio de Las Tunas a few kilometres from the road head. The descent and ascent of Friar's Col is semi-technical, requiring ropes and helmet. For the Rio Azufre and Friar's Col routes it is necessary to hire mules from the army. The army service is excellent. They will accommodate you and feed you at the road head, make great fires, take good care of the mules and act as guides. However, the service is slow and very expensive.

The routes to the summit via Rio Colorado and Friar's Col join on the mountain to ascend on the southern side of Tupungato. The other two routes join to ascend on the northern side of the mountain.

The shortest, and most popular, route up Tupungato, via Rio Colorado, is described here. Many guides and expedition operators in Santiago will organise the trek. The cost of transport from Santiago, and of hiring mules, is about half that for Aconcagua. **Three free permits** are required. In Santiago, on Bandera 52, the first permit is obtained from Dirección de Fronteras y Limites (DIFROL) and the second from the army office on Calle Santo Domingo. AES Gener, at Miraflores 222, operate the power station on the Rio Colorado and issue the final permit. The sequence is important. DIFROL should be the first stop – they will give you a note and directions to the army – and AES Gener the last. All this can now be arranged by email. If you email DIFROL first, their permit will detail the other email addresses to be contacted but you will need to bring your passport for the physical checks with the army and AES Gener.

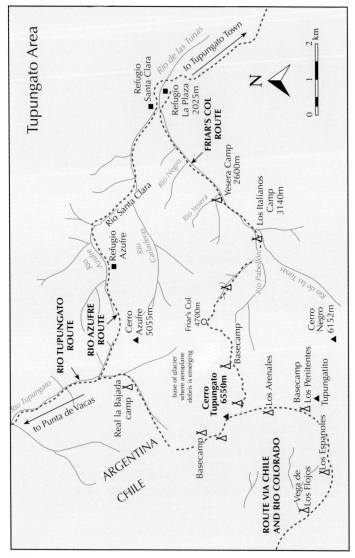

Tupungato Area

to Tupungato Town

Rio de las Tunas

Refugio Santa Clara

Refugio La Plaza 2025m

FRIAR'S COL ROUTE

Rio Negro

Rio Santa Clara

Yesera Camp 2600m

Los Italianos Camp 3140m

Rio Yesera

Refugio Azufre

Rio Carladeras

Rio Azufre

Rio Pabellón

Rio de las Tunas

RIO TUPUNGATO ROUTE

RIO AZUFRE ROUTE

▲ Cerro Azufre 5055m

Friar's Col 4700m

▲ Cerro Negro 6152m

Real la Bajada camp

base of glacier where aeroplane debris is emerging

Cerro Tupungato 6550m

Basecamp

Rio Tupungato

to Punta de Vacas

Los Arenales

Basecamp Los Penitentes Tupungatito

Basecamp

ARGENTINA

Los Espanoles

CHILE

Vega de Los Flojos

ROUTE VIA CHILE AND RIO COLORADO

N

0   1   2 km

Tupungato via Chile and Rio Colorado

Time	12 days
Distance	96km round trip
Terrain	Varied
Maximum elevation	6550m
Total climb	5000m
Water sources	Good

From Santiago the route is via the Cajón de Maipo, southeast of Santiago, through Las Vizcachas, La Obra and El Manzano. You must go into San José de Maipo to the army base to have your papers checked and stamped, and then proceed to the gates of AES Gener at Alfalfal. It is then 25km of dirt track road up to the start of the trek at Chacayal. En route you will pass arriero huts where you can hire mules. The dusty road is very busy with lorries from the open cast mine across the river from Chacayal.

At Chacayal there are good places to camp on grass and there is clean water. You may notice the many holes in the ground here, and you will see them again between Baños Azules and Vega de Los Flojos. These are made by little black moles, which make or clean out their burrows in the early morning. On this side of the Andes the flora is somewhat different to the Argentinean side, and there will be no chance of seeing guanacos.

The trail from Chacayal is along the right hand, southern bank of the Rio Colorado, along narrow precipitous paths, high above the raging river below. ▶ The first campsite is short of the **Rio Museo** (2400m). Known as **Baños Azules**, the site lies under the peak of Pan de Azucar (Bread of Sugar). The water running over the bare rock beside the campsite is heavy in minerals and not suitable for drinking, but there is good water below the campsite and further along the trail.

This initial stretch of 13km requires steady nerves and sure footings.

113

Day 1	Santiago to Chacayal and on to Baños Azules
Day 2	Baños Azules to Vega de los Flojos
Day 3	Vega de los Flojos to Basecamp Los Penitentes
Day 4	Rest day
Day 5	Carry to Camp 1 and return
Day 6	Move to Camp 1
Day 7	Carry to Camp Alto, Los Arenales, and return
Day 8	Move to Los Arenales
Day 9	Summit day and descend to Basecamp
Day 10	Spare Day
Day 11	Basecamp to Piedra Azul
Day 12	Piedra Azul to Santiago

Have your shell jacket ready in the rucksack for the trek from Baños Azules to Vega de los Flojos, and expect rain.

The second day is a 20km trek to Vega de los Flojos (3300m), a tough climb of 900m. ◀ Leaving Baños Azules the trail rises and falls to cross over the Rio Museo via a wooden bridge. Crossing the **Rio Azufre** is energy sapping, with three ascents and one descent to make. There were no bridges over the Rio Museo or the Rio Azufre until the arrieros constructed makeshift crossings as recently as 2006.

Once the rivers are crossed the trail is relatively uniform until you reach the base of **Piedra Azul**. This is an alternative campsite an hour or so short of Vega de los Flojos, perched above a mound of basalt, where the arrieros have built a shelter under a rock overhang. The campsite enjoys a wonderful view of Tupungato, but

The 'new' bridge over the Rio Azufre

the disadvantage is that you will get wet in the morning crossing the Rio Tupungatito. Going all the way to Vega de los Flojos allows for clothes that get wet in the river to dry out in the afternoon, ready for the morning.

One further point to consider is that it is not unusual for clouds to build up in the afternoons between Baños Azules and Vega de los Flojos, resulting in no sighting of Tupungato. Camping at Piedra Azul would ensure a wonderful vista of Tupungato in the early morning.

Perhaps in time the arrieros will build a bridge over the Rio Tupungatito, but in 2009 there was still none, and the crossing at **Mal Paso** is an exciting, quite precarious, event. **Vega de los Flojos** (spring of the loose rocks/ground) is a green area, somewhat similar to Piedra Numerada on the El Plomo trek. At 3300m it is relatively well sheltered and has good water nearby, but there is no view of the mountain. You will have noticed the cattle and horses that graze between Baños Azules and Mal Paso, and wondered how they got there. The path from Chacayal to Baños Azules is hardly suitable for large animals.

From Baños Azules to the summit of Tupungato there are multiple campsites to choose from. Above Vega de los Flojos most climbers to make their basecamp at **Los Penitentes** (4400m), however, there are choices below that, such as at **Los Espanoles** (4000m). There is no water available here, but there is at Los Penitentes. ▶ Above Los Penitentes it is usual to make Camp 1 at 5200m, and a second camp at **Los Arenales** (5900m).

As its name suggests, Los Penitentes is distinguishable by the many penitentes nearby.

Summit day from Los Arenales is only 650m, and is not taxing as summit days go. Expect the day to be extremely windy, with a severe wind chill effect. There are no difficult or technical obstacles to overcome en route.

As the final surge to the summit is short, there should be time to break camp and descend to basecamp on the same day. The next day can be short or long as desired. Some just cross the river below Vega de los Flojos, make camp at Piedra Azul to dry out, and enjoy a last look at the mountain in the morning. Others make haste as far as Baños Azules.

On the way down there are significant ascents and descents required to cross Rio Azufre.

TUPUNGATO PROVINCIAL PARK

On the Argentinean side the Tupungato Provincial Park (170,000ha) stretches along the Chilean border south of the Mendoza-to-Santiago road. More extensive than the Aconcagua Provincial Park (150,000ha), it is a wild, remote region. Herds of guanacos roam freely. Condors soar overhead.

Access to the southern side of the park is usually via the RN 40 road south out of Mendoza, and turning right onto the RP 86 to the town of Tupungato, a journey of 80km. There are daily buses from Santiago to Tupungato town. From the road, looking across the plain, there is a

The start of Friar's Col is steep and may be covered in snow

spectacular view of the Andes from the Frontal Cordillera with El Plata (6300m) to the Principal Cordillera and Tupungato (6550m).

The charming, friendly town of Tupungato has much to offer the traveller – trekking, horse trekking, wineries, fly fishing, to name but a few. Above all else it is a peaceful place. At an elevation of 1050m it is not quite as warm as Mendoza, and is subject to snow in the winter. There are two good and inexpensive hotels, both on the main street, with the tourist office in the foyer of one of them.

It is necessary to obtain permission from the army to enter the park. The army camp in Tupungato town issues the permit, which is free. From the camp it is 35km over dirt road to where the road divides – to the left and south Refugio La Plaza, to the right and north Refugio Santa Clara.

There are three refugios in this area, all initially intended as hostels for trekkers, now all army camps. Refugio Plaza is the nearest to Tupungato town and the starting point for the trek via Friar's Col. Over the Rio de las Tunas, a few kilometres further on, is Refugio Santa Clara. The dirt track carries on past Santa Clara for a further 20km to Refugio Azufre, the starting point for the trek via Rio Azufre.

Wilderness trek to Friar's Col

Time	5 to 7-day trek
Distance	70km round trip
Terrain	Varied
Maximum elevation	4700m
Total climb	2675m
Water sources	Yes

It is highly unlikely that you will meet anyone on this trek – only a few parties each year seek a permit. Wild guanacos will be seen quite often. Condors and many other birds, lizards and mice, possibly a fox are all most likely. A fire can be lit every night; there is plenty of water and good places to camp. Binoculars will be valuable for locating guanacos and condors, and for spotting pieces of the crashed aeroplane when looking across from Friar's Col to Tupungato.

The goal is to climb to an elevation of 4700m at the Portezuelo del Fraile (Friar's Col), a prominent vantage point from where there are spectacular views of Tupungato and its glacier, and a panorama of the Andes over to Aconcagua. The route can also be used to climb Tupungato itself, as long as you are prepared for the difficult descent and ascent of Friar's Col.

Transport must be arranged from the town of Tupungato, where you will have obtained a permit from the army camp, to Refugio La Plaza. If mules have been hired from the army they will arrange transport to the refugio. The army will offer the options of delivering a load to the first or second campsite, taking trekkers in by mule, guiding them and taking them out, or providing pack mules and a ride to a point on the trail. The option of hiring a mule only from the army is unlikely to be acceptable.

At **Refugio La Plaza** (2025m), the soldiers will be welcoming, probably offering food and accommodation. What is possibly more important is to ask for a ride over the river **Rio de Las Tunas**. This fast-flowing river is down a gorge, and must be crossed at the start of the trek.

Day 1

Following the right hand bank of the river, through the gorge, the route leads over a grassy plain and up into the valley. The snow-capped peak ahead is Cerro Negro (6152m). The river is murky, a faded orange colour. The route over the next few days will be to follow the orange river, and when a fork in the river is encountered take the right hand branch. This will lead eventually up to Friar's Col. The colour of the water is due to sulphur (azufre) deposits further up the mountain.

The **Yesera camp** is 10km from La Plaza and at a height of 2600m. It is found immediately after crossing a stream (**Rio Yesera**), where there is clear water. Look out for a landmark concrete slab and a timber upright – the remnants of a former refugio built in the days of Juan Peron. There will be a store of firewood near the designated fireplace. ◀

It is the custom on campsites to leave behind adequate firewood, so that trekkers arriving late do not have to search in the dark. Even if the stock is high, replenish it.

If 10km on the first day is not enough for you, the second campsite is 15km further on, with an alternative site a further 5km still.

Day 2

The trail continues along the right hand bank of the Rio de las Tunas until it meets the **Rio Pabellón**. Now the Pabellón takes on the orange colour, and comes down from a valley to the right. Beyond the junction of the two rivers it is necessary to cross to the left-hand bank, where camp **Los Italianos** is situated (3140m). The snow-capped peak now up ahead is Cerro Pabellón (6100m). Firewood can be found up the hills. Around the camp there are tufts of bright green dense vegetation, some turning brown. This is yareta, which turns brown when it dies and makes good fuel for the fire. Water from the river is murky but drinkable.

The energetic may decide to proceed on past Los Italianos to a campsite 5km further on. Casa del Cura is nestled under an overhanging rock, affording good shelter if the weather is bad.

Day 3

This is guanaco day, so tread lightly and have zoom lenses at the ready. The route is along the left bank of the Rio Pabellón until it meets the Rio Ancha, then turn right up Arroyo de la Quebrada Ancha (stream of the wide valley). The trail becomes steeper and the start of the col can be seen ahead. It is wise to be prepared, for the col continues for 7–8 km up to the vantage point.

A camp can be made below the first step of the col at 3600m, or, if the weather is kind, up above the first step at 4200m. The first step of the col is steep and may be covered in snow, in which case crampons are required. Above this first step there is no water and no firewood.

Day 4

From below the first step of the col to the vantage point is 4–5hrs and 2hrs back. Just a daypack is required. Passing through the long windy col over rocky ground will be slow. The dip in the ridge up ahead is the vantage point (4700m). There is even a place to pitch a tent here, though it would be extremely windy.

There is no view of Tupungato, or any other mountain until one arrives at the vantage point, where suddenly an amazing vista opens up over the awesome mass of Tupungato. The glacier that conceals the remains of the crashed Lancaster can be seen clearly, and it is obvious how difficult it would be to find a diamond at the foot of the glacier – which is 8km long and perhaps 2km wide. Off to the northwest is Aconcagua; between it and Tupungato is El Plata (6300m).

The descent down **Friar's Col** is 100m of an almost vertical drop over loose rock. A pair of helmeted climbers, alternating with a rope, could manage to descend, but the subsequent ascent with a heavy pack would be difficult and dangerous.

Days 5 and 6

Retrace your route back to La Plaza. This can comfortably be achieved in two days.

El Morado Valley with springs in the foreground and
Cerro Morado at 4500m defining the end of the valley

PART 4
SANTIAGO AREA

SANTIAGO

SANTIAGO CITY

A third of the population of Chile, some five million people, live in this sprawling metropolis. The centre of the city is compact – it is easy to orientate yourself – and has an excellent underground metro. The outer suburbs, however, are disjointed and it is remarkably easy to get lost.

On a clear morning Santiago, viewed from the west, is dwarfed by the snow-capped cordillera of the Andes. During winter, however, it is one of the most polluted cities in the world, as the mountains can prevent the smog from clearing.

Santiago has a more complex layout than Mendoza. The Rio Mapocho carves the city in two in an east–west direction. The main street of Santiago is Avenida del Libertador Bernardo O'Higgins, also commonly known, as in Mendoza, as the Alameda. The great liberator O'Higgins himself gave this name to it when he ordered the planting of trees to form a French-style boulevard.

At the lowest point of the curve of the Rio Mapocho is Baquedano, which may be considered the city's hub. The road that goes west is the Pan American Route towards

Street scene in Santiago

Valparaiso. To the north is the airport and Argentina, and on the east lie the Andes.

Every hotel reception has city maps. The bustling, mainly pedestrianised, city centre lies to the north of the Alameda, between the metro stations of Universidad de Chile and Santa Lucia.

Public transport
Public transport in and around Santiago is excellent. The long distance buses arrive from Mendoza at Los Heroes station. This is also where the bus from the airport stops. From here there is a metro throughout the city and other bus connections to outer areas. It is much more convenient, and of course cheaper, to see Santiago and its nearby attractions by public transport than to hire a car and brave the traffic. Chilean drivers are undisciplined, swerving in and out of lanes and generally driving too fast.

The Santiago metro plan is easy enough to understand and has four lines, numbered 1 to 5, with no 3 missing. Los Heroes is at one junction, Baquedano is at another, and Tobolaba is at a third. Line no 4A is under construction and will circle the city to the southeast. Like all metros the directions are given as the last station on the line. The cost of a metro trip is one price irrespective of the distance.

Unlike Mendoza businesses do not close for siesta in Santiago.

Handling money
The Chilean peso is a different currency to the Argentinean peso, and has been more stable against the US dollar than its neighbour's. Like Mendoza, it is better to change money into Chilean pesos and pay for everything in the local currency. The rates are not as volatile as in Mendoza, and you can safely change money in hotel receptions, banks and at dedicated money exchange offices. If you are in Providencia there are two casas de cambio on Pedro de Valdivia.

For the mountaineer there are many gear shops in the city with everything that might be required for an expedition. The costs are a little higher than in Mendoza. There are a few outlets where gear may also be hired.

SURVIVAL TIP

Making international calls from hotels is very expensive. Most internet cafés provide a service that is 20 per cent of the cost, and there are specialist telephone call centres that are 10 per cent of hotel costs. These telephone call centres are generally at metro stations, for instance in the metro of Universidad de Chile, or at bus stations, where they may be labelled *casa de llamada*.

IN AND AROUND SANTIAGO

A trip from Baquedano north through Bellavista and up to the heights of San Cristobal (by funicular railway) is worthwhile. There is a good view of the city and the Andes from here. The zoo is en route.

Near metro station Cal y Canto, beside the river, or not to far from Plaza des Armes, there is the marvellous Mercado Central (Central Market). In the enormous steel-supported hall there is a wonderful fish restaurant. Not open in the evenings it is full every lunchtime, especially on Sundays, accommodating up to 800 diners. The menus include fish perhaps never seen in Western restaurants. All around are endless stalls selling fresh fish, fruit and vegetables. Originally intended to be a railway station, the art noveau steel structure of the Mercado Central was made in Belgium in 1872 and shipped to Santiago.

The El Plomo Inca Mummy, or at least a replica of it (see page 130), can be seen in the Museo de Historia Natural in the Quinta Normal Park, off Matacana (metro to Estación Central). It should be noted that some are sceptical of the mummy's authenticity, given that it was found in prime condition on such a well-visited mountain so close to the city, and only discovered in 1954.

A good centre to buy gifts for home is Plaza Artesanos de Manquehue, a series of small shops in a covered market on Manquehue Sur, off Av Apoquindo near Las Condes.

Lapis lazuli is Chile's semi precious stone, and necklaces, earrings and cuff links in silver and gold can be purchased here or in Bellavista. The airport shops charge roughly double for the same items.

From the junction of Alameda and Ahumeda in Santiago buses regularly go to the Maipo valley. This long picturesque valley stretches some 70 km into the mountains. There are small wineries for tasting, places to stop and purchase honey, cider and crafts en route, and at the top of the valley there are hot springs (see also the El Morado trek, page 125).

At the start of the Maipo Valley is the vineyard of Concha y Toro. Entrance is free and it is a most

Replica of the El Plomo mummy

rewarding experience. The best time to visit is at 10am when there is an English language tour and it is still cool. Each participant is given a free tasting glass, allowed to sample three top wines and taken through the vineyard and its cellars. Concha y Toro is renowned for the quality of its *carmanére reserva*.

Many of Chile's notable wineries are not as easily accessible as in Mendoza. Undurraga, however, one of the oldest and most prestigious wineries in Chile, is only 35km away,

at Melpilla on the road towards San Antonio, southwest of Santiago. Their dessert wine, which is referred to as 'late harvest', is particularly delicious.

A 1½ hr bus journey from the bus station at the University of Santiago takes you to Valparaiso and the coastal resort of Viña del Mar. It can be particularly refreshing to take a walk by the sea after weeks in the mountains. Valparaiso is a quaint old port town with 15 old funicular railways. On Sundays there is an enormous flea market.

CHILEAN RODEOS

Every weekend throughout the summer there are rodeos in or near Santiago. To attend a rodeo is to witness a part of the life of Chile. For the purists, Rancagua, the city some 90km south of Santiago, is the home of the Chilean rodeo, and draws bigger crowds to its events. However, the rodeos in and around Santiago give a good flavour of the occasion. In the Friday and Saturday press details of the rodeos are listed in the sports events of the weekend. The rodeo season begins in September, starting with qualifying events, and finishes with regional finals, semi-finals and the grand final in March.

The rodeo is quite different from its North American counterpart. The Chilean version is essentially about horsemanship. There is no wrestling with bulls or bringing calves to earth. Huasos, dressed elegantly with wide-brimmed hats, ponchos and high boots, and working in pairs, chase and control young cows using only their horses. There are no ropes, no whips, and no animal abuse. This is a display of skill and elegance. The judges award points for dressage and for the efficiency with which the Huasos control the cattle.

ROUTES NEAR SANTIAGO

El Morado valley

Time	Half day
Distance	15km round trip
Terrain	Easy
Maximum elevation	2450m
Total climb	650m
Water source	Yes

Walking shoes only are required on this walk, which is at a relatively low altitude. El Morado is a national park within the Maipo valley, and this walk is a popular one for Santiaginos at the weekends. The route is through a picturesque valley, where there are many campsites, past natural springs, lots of flowers, particularly orchids, up to a glacier.

Transport to El Morado during weekdays must be arranged. At weekends there are early morning minibuses (7am) from Plaza Italia. Public buses go up the Maipo valley, but stop short of Baños Morales, where the walk starts. The La Cumbre gear shop on Apoquindo is associated with an outdoor sports centre, Refugio Valdes, which is located at Baños Morales, and may be able to help. This centre, incidentally, not only arranges treks, but also has a full range of outdoor activities including horse trekking, fossil hunting, rock climbing and mountain biking.

Through the Maipo valley, passing sports and recreation areas, wineries, waterfalls and stunning countryside, the road goes through San José de Maipo onto a dirt track to branch off for Baños Morales. The lukewarm springs in the village are worth a visit.

There is a small fee for entry into the park, payable to the park ranger at the entrance. Initially the path is steep, but then it levels to an even gradient. En route one cannot fail to notice the profusion of flowers. Orchids and calandrinias are particularly plentiful. A drink from the sulphur springs beside the path will refresh (just a little – the taste may linger). The path eventually leads into a flat campsite beside a number of lagoons.

Cerro Morado (4500m) is the jagged peak at the end of the valley. To its left is Cerro San Francisco (4350m) that has a glacier, which sweeps down to discharge its morainic load beside the path, at an altitude of 2450m.

La Campana national park

There are two approaches to visiting this national park:
- for a gruelling 1400m climb over granite rock in the hot sun, or
- for a sightseeing walk through a forest where there are many of the rare Chilean palms.

Whichever you take, the park is an enjoyable day trip from Santiago. There are many species of birds and plants in this wildlife sanctuary.

La Campana is a national park that lies between Santiago and Valparaiso. It is part of the coastal cordillera ridge of mountains. The dominant peak that can be seen from every part of the park is Cerro La Campana (1880m).

There are two entrances to La Campana national park, quite distinct and separate. To climb the peak use the entrance near Olmué, on the western side. (You will not see the palms on this route.)

Near Ocoa, on the northern side there is a second entrance that is close to the palms, but two days' trek to Cerro La Campana. Ocoa is 1½hrs by car from Santiago, and a further hour by public bus. Olmué is 2hrs by car and 3hrs by public bus. The buses to Ocoa do no go to the park entrances, but stop approximately 2km short. Buses from San Borja near Estación Central in Santiago go very close to the Olmué park entrance.

At both park entrances there are clear maps displaying the various trails through the forest, where the palms are and where the campsites are located. A small entrance fee is payable, with an additional cost to camp.

One of the very early visitors to La Campana was Charles Darwin in 1834. He climbed Cerro La Campana (on a cool winter's day) and was overwhelmed by the 360° vista of the Pacific Ocean around to the Andes.

The Chilean palm was widespread in Central Chile until it was discovered that it contained a vast store of delicious treacle. Felling of the trees for its treacle was set upon with a will, and, as a result, the tree became almost extinct. It is now protected, and La Campana is the only significant source to survive. The massive trunks are often compared to elephant's legs. Very small coconuts are produced.

The humming bird and the inquisitive truca, with its distinctive call, are birds that flourish in this natural habitat.

El Plomo 5430m

Cerro el Plomo, translated as The Mountain of Lead, is the nearest 5000m peak to Santiago, and its white-capped summit can be seen from all parts of the city. The non-technical climb is the most popular in Chile, attracting thousands of trekkers every season. It gets its name from the deposits of lead that were mined in the area.

No permit is required and no permissions are necessary. Nor do you need a guide. The route is clear and the dangers are few. There will be others on the mountain.

As part of preparations for Aconcagua, El Plomo has much to offer:
- the ground conditions are very similar for both mountains
- crampons will be required to cross the glacier near the summit
- summit day is a long arduous day, with possibly 1330m of climbing

The trek takes 4–5 days round trip from Santiago. Those with some acclimatisation will have no difficulty

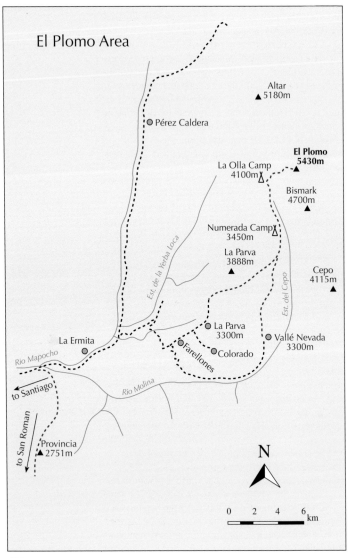

El Plomo Area

Altar
▲ 5180m

● Pérez Caldera

El Plomo
5430m
▲

La Olla Camp
4100m ⋀

Bismark
4700m
▲

Numerada Camp ⋀
3450m

La Parva
3888m
▲

Cepo
4115m
▲

La Parva
3300m ●

● Vallé Nevada
3300m

La Ermita
●

● Farellones

● Colorado

Río Mapocho

Est. de la Yerba Loca

Est. del Cepo

to Santiago

Río Molina

to San Roman

Provincia
▲ 2751m

N

0   2   4   6 km

in a four-day, or possibly even a three-day, trek. For those preparing for Aconcagua or Tupungato an extra day at altitude will be most beneficial.

A number of operators organise guided expeditions up El Plomo, complete with mules. Indeed, some offer the package of El Plomo and Aconcagua as two peaks in two countries, El Plomo intended as acclimatisation for Aconcagua. It is the custom with some of these operators to concentrate the expedition into four days, so that the summit day includes the trek back to the first camp. This is too onerous, even for those acclimatised.

Time	4–5 days
Distance	40km round trip
Terrain	Varied
Maximum elevation	5430m
Total climb	2400m
Water sources	Yes

The mountain lies 20km to the northeast of Santiago, and is accessed via the valley of the Mapocho river. There are two alternative starting points, both at ski resorts, both at approximately the same altitude, and both requiring a car for access. Public buses go from the centre of Santiago (Escuela Militar metro station or Alameda) via Las Condes towards Barnecha. However, these buses will not travel in far enough to the trailhead. If a group is going a shared taxi will be economical. For those on their own there is a custom of hitching in the area, which will be much more successful at weekends.

The route out of Santiago is via Las Condes and the rather affluent suburb of Vitacura, then into the Mapocho valley, passing the exclusive houses of Arrayan. The starting point at La Parva ski resort is on the road beyond Farallones. For the Valle Nevada starting point the road rises steeply after the copper mine, and after numerous hairpin bends arrives at one of Chile's most popular ski centres. At both ski resorts there are hotels, one of which remains open throughout the year. These hotels cater for day-trippers and those seeking peace and relief from the heat of Santiago. They are expensive.

The trails from both starting points join together after a few kilometres to become one trail in to the first camp-site. The mules leave from beside the hotels.

Day 1

Whether from La Parva or Valle Nevada the route begins at an altitude of 3300m. In the summer it will be possible for the delivery car or truck to go up the ski roads to shorten the first day's trek, but this may not be such a good policy for those seeking acclimatisation. The trek in to the first campsite at Piedra Numerada is a mere 3hrs, initially over steep ground, levelling and falling into the camp. From Valle Nevada the route goes directly up the ski slopes, around various reservoirs, following the main river valley.

> **Piedra Numerada** is at an elevation of 3450m, not much height gain from the ski centre. It is on an open plain, beside the Molina river, and there is room here for in excess of 50 tents. Cerro El Plomo can be seen clearly up the valley. To the right, dominating the campsite is Cerro Bismarck (4700m). The climb up Bismarck is very steep and demanding, but non-technical.

THE INCA MUMMY

At a height of 5200m there is an Inca altar. It is constructed of dry stone and has an enclosure beside it. Some 200m above the altar, on the summit plateau, there are three rectangular enclosures. In one of them the congealed body of a small boy was discovered in 1954. The body was dressed in fine fabrics of vicuna and alpaca, and wrapped in a blanket. His hair was braided, and on his feet were fine leather moccasins. It is thought that the boy was a sacrifice to the Inca gods. A replica of the mummified remains can be seen in the Museo de Historia Natural in the Quinta Normal Park off Matacana in Santiago.

In front of Piedra Numerada there are springs of refreshing spring water. Around the mighty boulder in the centre of the camp a dry stone wall has been constructed that makes an excellent kitchen. There are plenty of sierra thrushes and wrens about the camp, and the perdicitias call to each other all day.

The campsite at Piedra Numerada with El Plomo in the background

Day 2
From Piedra Numerada to the second campsite at La Olla (The Pot) is a 3hr walk over uneven moraine. The landscape becomes bleak and barren, with few plants and even fewer birds. En route there are the remains of an Inca enclosure.

Where to make camp at **La Olla** is a big decision. The best site is beside the orange Refugio Federación – no more than a tent-size wooden box – at 4100m. There is a water source here, the ground is flat and there is ample wind protection. However, it is 1330m to the summit, a mighty climb for one day.

All sites above Federación are devoid of water. The first is La Olla itself, over the moraine ridge and down to a level of 4200m – hardly worth the effort. At 4300m there is a small, sheltered site with room for six tents. It is on the trail up the mountain. Finally, at 4600m, beside a dilapidated timber hut, Refugio Agostini, there are a few spaces for tents, but the site is very exposed. In calm weather this site would be a good option.

A day acclimatising at La Olla may pay dividends, but any site above Federación is confined and could be exposed and windy.

Day 3/4

From Federación or La Olla summit day should commence at 3 to 4am. This is aimed at reaching the summit at mid-day when the weather conditions tend to be more favourable. Since the climb will start in the darkness it is good practice to become acquainted with the lower part of it the evening before.

Initially the route is easy. The approach to Agostini, however, is over loose scree (acarreo). Leaving Agostini the ground improves slightly, but then deteriorates to resemble Aconcagua's Canaleta. The scree underfoot is weak and makes climbing frustrating. The last hour of the El Plomo climb is over a glacier in crampons

Before the dawn breaks, a look back at the lights of Santiago will make for a welcome pause.

The amount of snow on the mountain will dictate the difficulty of the ascent to the site of the altar. Over a slope that is sheltered from the sun, compact snow or ice may require crampons, but will be easier to climb. If there is no snow or ice the ground underfoot will be loose.

The site of the sacrifice altar is a moving experience. One imagines the trauma on the mountain, 500 years ago, when a family gave up their little son for the common good. From the altar to the summit is a climb in crampons over the glacier. It is possible to shorten the time on the glacier by a roundabout route over stony ground – either way the climb is over an hour, although at first sight it looks like half of this. There is a relatively flat ridge along the summit plateau of El Plomo, several hundred metres long. A simple wooden cross marks the highest point. On a clear day there are stunning views of Tupungato (6550m), Marmolejo (6110m) and Aconcagua (6962m).

Delight and relief at the summit of El Plomo

Day 4/5
An early start the day after summit day allows adequate time to get back to the ski resort and into Santiago by nightfall. The walk is long and the final climb over the hills to the ski slopes will be taxing after the previous day's exertions. The hotel at the ski resort is quite used to serving dirty, unshaven climbers.

Hotel at the start of the El Plomo trek at Valle Nevada

Provincia and San Roman

Along the road in towards El Plomo, just before the bridge over the Mapocho, Puente Lihue, there is a sign, Camino de Naranjo, pointing to the south. This is the start of a trail that goes over Cerro Provincia (2751m), and on to Cerro San Ramón (3249m). It is 5hrs trek from the road to the top of Cerro Provincia, and another 5hrs to the summit of Cerro San Ramón.

These are serious climbs that will necessitate camping, and will require heavy backpacks to be taken from 1100m at the road up to these peaks. On a cool day, however, it is possible to climb and descend in one day. The route is well marked out, but be advised that there are a few false summits before the top.

From either of these peaks there should be, subject to weather conditions, good views of the city, probably giving a good impression of the smog that the Andes manages to trap.

APPENDIX 1
Maps, guidebooks and further reading

Maps

Until very recently the availability of accurate ordnance maps of Aconcagua was poor, and was non-existent until 2003. However, in 2005 Aoneker GIS Solutions published an accurate topographical map of Aconcagua. It comes in 1:50,000 and in 1:100,000 versions. Not that easy to source, you will certainly spot it on the wall in reception of the hotel in Los Penitentes, and they usually have copies for sale.

There still exist various photomaps of the mountain with the various features marked on an aerial picture. The best of these is a 1:50,000 version, published by World's End, on sale at Mendoza airport. Inka Expeditions published a map, but it is surpassed by the new map referred to above.

A 1:50,000 map of Aconcagua is published by Cordee of Leicester, England. The map shows the Normal route only, but its accuracy has been questioned.

The South American Explorers Club publishes a small map in black and white, entitled Aconcagua – Summit of the Americas by Ed Darack. It has useful data, but is a poor substitute for a proper map.

Guidebooks and further reading

RJ Secor's *Aconcagua – A Climbing Guide*, published in the US by The Mountaineers (first published in 1994), is an old guidebook with many black and white photographs.

Aconcagua – Summit of the Andes (2006), written by an Argentinean high mountain guide, Mauricio Fernandez, is a worthwhile read.

The Bradt Trekking Guide to Chile and Argentina by Tim Burford contains a nine-page chapter on Aconcagua.

Franz Schubert and Malte Sieber, German climbers living in Chile, published *Adventure Handbook – Central Chile* (2002), documenting 23 trekking tours in the Chilean Andes, and published by Viachile Editores, it may not be readily available in the west.

The Rough Guides are great for getting around: *Chile and Argentina: The Rough Guide to Argentina* by Danny Aeberhard, Andrew Benson, Rosalba O'Brien and Lucy Phillips (2008); *The Rough Guide to Chile* by Melissa Graham and Andrew Benson (2006).

Wayne Bernhardson is the author of an excellent guide to Chile which is part of the Moon Handbooks series.

The Highest Alps – A Record of the First Ascent of Aconcagua and Tupungato and the Exploration of the Surrounding Valleys, by EA Fitzgerald (1899), published by Methuen, is a wonderful study of the area, despite its age.

Geology of the Cordillera Principal, by Victor Ramos (Secretaria de Mineria de la Nación, Argentina, 1994). *Geologica de la Region de Aconcagua*, Victor Ramos (Dir Nac De Servicio Geologica, 1996) – a larger, comprehensive treatise in Spanish.

APPENDIX 2
Guides and mountain services

The Mendoza local government website on Aconcagua gives a list of companies who provide services within the national park, complete with addresses, websites and telephone numbers.

- Aconcagua Guides and Services
- Aconcagua Expediciones
- Aconcagua Express
- Andesport
- Aymara Aventuras & Expediciones
- Campo Base Travel & Adventure
- Cumbres Argentina
- Fernando Grajales
- Expeditions Geotrek
- Inka Expediciones
- Juan Herrera Travel Services
- Lanko Altas Montañas
- Mallku Expediciones
- MDQ Expediciones
- Refugio Plaza de Mulas
- Viajes Ghisolfi
- Xperience Aconcagua

They include only Argentinean companies based in Mendoza. Three Chilean companies, Azimuth360, Chile Montana and Aventuras Patagonicas are very experienced on Aconcagua. There is a fourth, KL Adventure, based in Santiago that organises expeditions, skiing and trekking.

The three largest expedition operators are Fernando Grajales, Aymara and Inka Expediciones. Grajales is a second generation operator. His father, a renowned former climber, was the first to set up services on Aconcagua. With a stock of over 90 mules Grajales provides a range of commercial services, including mules and the hire of mess tents, complete with cooks. Grajales hires guides to suit his bookings.

Aymara is a large company providing leisure and entertainment services throughout Argentina. They hire mules and guides to fit their needs. Aymara will carry gear, so that the climber only has to carry his own small daypack. This may seem like a useful luxury, but can be counterproductive in the acclimatisation process. The only time when a porter is valuable is on the descent to basecamp.

Inka Expediciones has a stock of over 60 mules, and a permanent team of more than 40 top class guides at the height of the season. Whereas many of Grajales' guides and some of Aymara's are accomplished, but not licensed, Inka appears to be very particular, only employing guides who are licensed. Inka is affiliated to the international mountain leader organisation UIAGM, the first company on Aconcagua to do so. It is also a partner in the Leave No Trace world federation. In preparing for an expedition Inka's response time was found to be excellent. The reputation of two Chilean operators, Chile Montana and Azimuth360, is also very good.

APPENDIX 3

Accommodation and local facilities

SOME LOCAL TERMINOLOGY	
Hotel	Bathroom en suite, stars awarded by the hotel itself, breakfast always included
Suite Hotel or **Aparthotel**	Hotel with a kitchen, no breakfast
Hospedaje	Similar to a hotel, but no single rooms, no room telephones, or televisions, basic facilities, breakfast
Hostería	No en-suite bathrooms, basic facilities, no breakfast
Cabaña	Self catering accommodation, usually a wooden house
Alberque	Large dormitory style accommodation, not necessarily including breakfast

Set out below is a non-exhaustive list of hotels where the author has been and stayed. In the major cities there are many hundreds of other such hotels.

The Rough Guides are good references for information on transport and places to stay, but for places to eat it is essential to have the most up-to-date edition.

MENDOZA

Electricity is 220V/50Hz, with two-pin combination sockets, which will take a normal Western two-pin plug. Near the permit office, off the main street, on Garibaldi, is a tourist office. The post offices are called Correo and to make a telephone call the Locutorio are inexpensive and efficient. The latter also have cheap and efficient internet facilities.

The unit of currency is the Argentinean peso, but $US are also accepted. Smaller denomination $US are useful, as it is difficult to obtain change in $US. The peso exchange rate to the dollar has varied from parity in 1999 to 4 to 1 in 2003. In 2009 the exchange rate stood at 3.45 to the $US. (See also 'Changing Money and Paying for Things'.)

Places to stay

There are numerous hotels in Mendoza, from budget to medium priced to luxurious. Inflation has driven the costs per night up considerably over the past few years, so you must now expect to pay Western prices.

Here is a selection of 3-star hotels you can book online. All have free internet access in their lobbies and they are all generally about the same cost. The aparthotels and suite hotels will have a kitchen where you can cook for yourself.

- Hotel Provincial, Belgrano 1259
- Park Suites Aparthotel, Av Mitre 753
- El Portal Suites Aparthotel, Necochea 661
- El Condor Suite Hotel, Leonidas Aguirre 90
- Villagio Hotel, 25 de Mayo 1010
- Montañas Azul ApartHotel, on Peru near Plaza Chile

The Villagio Hotel, and the Montanas Azul Aparthotel are a little more expensive than the others, and are close to the main square, Plaza Independencia. There are plenty of cafés and restaurants in the neighbourhood, such as on the Paseo Sarmiento, a pedestrianised street leading off Plaza Independencia. On the same street as the Villagio, the 25 de Mayo, is the slightly cheaper Corolla Hotel, and the Princess Hotel. On Perú, the same street as the Montanas Azul, is the Zamara Hotel, an old style establishment situated between Espejo and Sarmiento.

If you prefer to be as close to the action as possible, and to stay in a cheap, clean, no nonsense hotel, then Hotel Puerta del Sol is a two star, low budget hotel just around the corner from the permit office and the main street. It is on Garibaldi, off Av

San Martin. There is no room safe, no internet, and an old fashioned lift. Across the street is a no-nonsense cheap eating house. Very similar is the Royal Hotel Horcones, on Las Heras 159.

For low budget travellers, next door to El Portal Suites is the Windsor Hotel, and around the corner are the Petit and the Kapac hotels. This area of Mendoza is very quiet and is close to restaurants and the permit office.

Hosteling Internacional on Espana 343, Hostel Campo Base on Mitre 946, and Hostel Independencia on Mitre 1247, are all alternative low budget hostels.

The Hotel Aconcagua on San Lorenzo 545 is an example of an up-market establishment. Approximately 25 per cent more expensive than the 3-star hotels, it teems with north Americans, many on the Aconcagua trail. If you want to stay in the height of luxury you can check out the Park Hyatt on Chile, facing the main park of Plaza Independencia.

Eating out

La Florencia on the corner of Sarmiento and Perú is possibly Mendoza's best restaurant. It is not expensive, and the quality of its food is excellent. The restaurant has its own ranch where the meat is brought from. There is clear glass between the kitchen and the street, so you can see the food being prepared from the tables outside. Their bife chorizo may rival the best steak you are ever likely to eat. If it is full there are reasonable substitutes down and across the street.

There are a number of large restaurants in the city where there is a set charge and no limitation on how much you can eat. Las Tinajas on Lavalle 38 and Caro Pepe on Las Heras near Chile are examples.

Also on Las Heras at 485, across the street from Caro Pepe, is De un Rincón, a good quality, quiet restaurant. Further along Las Heras at 596 there is the lively Mediterráneo.

On Villanueva between Parque General San Martin and Belgrano there are many restaurants, for example Torcuato, an expensive establishment that serves great food.

On Belgrano near Sarmiento there is a fine restaurant called Lasal, with an extensive list of the best wines made in Mendoza.

There are two MacDonald's, one on Av San Martin near Garibaldi, the other on Las Heras at Mendocinos.

The permit office in Mendoza

Shops

Av San Martin, the lower end of Las Heras, and Paseo Sarmiento are the main shopping streets. There are two Carrefour Supermarkets, one at the end of Belgrano at the junction with Las Heras, the second on Las Heras at Mendocinos.

Mountain equipment

Whereas a few years ago there were only a few outlets selling and hiring mountain equipment, the city is now teeming with them. However, costs are no longer cheap and compare with Western prices.

Hiring equipment includes the full range from crampons, double plastic boots, tents, down jackets and sleeping bags to cooking stoves and camping utensils. Rental costs are approximately ten per cent of the purchase price per day, or 25 per cent for 20 days. A credit guarantee is required. For expeditions deals can be struck for an all-inclusive price. At the height of the season in 2009 the

FOREIGN EMBASSIES IN MENDOZA		
Brazil Peru 789 ☎ 423 1422	**Israel** Lamadrid 738 ☎ 427 1507	**Slovenia** Roberto Ortiz (Godoy Cruz) ☎ 427 1986
Denmark Agustin Alvarez 555 ☎ 423 2610	**Italy** Necocea 712 ☎ 423 1640	**Spain** Agustin Alvarez 455 ☎ 438 3947
Finland Lujan de Cuyo ☎ 498 5509	**Portugal** Guaymallen ☎ 451 4179	**Syria** Av San Martin 1786 ☎ 423 4063
France Houssay 790 ☎ 423 1542	**Romania** San Jose ☎ 431 7020	
Germany Montevideo 127 ☎ 429 6539	**San Marino** Espejo 79 ☎ 423 5383	

outlets still had a reasonable selection of gear for hire.

Orviz is located at Juan B. Gusto 536 (close to Inka Expediciones). About 100m away on the continuation of Juan B. Justo, Las Heras (close to 25 de Mayo) is Aconcagua 6962. You can compare prices by walking between the two.

Limite Vertical is on Sarmiento 675. El Refugio Adventure Equipment is at Peatonal Sarmiento 294, in the city centre at Plaza Independencia.

Wineries

Mendoza is the heart of the Argentinean wine industry, and it is not far from the city centre to the vineyards. There is an excellent book entitled Wine Routes of Argentina written

by Alan Young, an Australian living in California.

The choice of vineyards is enormous. English is spoken at all of them and wine tours are constantly in progress, though the mornings may be better. The Weinert Winery is close to Casa Fader. Chandon, Etchart, Trapiche, Finca Flinchman and Norton are other choices with international reputations.

These are some of the big names in Argentina wine, but some of the smaller vineyards are worth a visit too. They will generally not speak English, but have a surprisingly varied choice. Although malbec is the grape that Argentina has become synonymous with, these smaller vineyards produce wines from such other grapes as tokay, barbera and bonarda. The harsher grape varieties native to Argentina (and ones to be generally avoided), are criolla grande and cereza.

Ampora Wine Tours on Sarmiento 647, and Trout and Wine, organise set wine tours. Some of these take in a tasting lunch where you sample wines chosen to compliment various foods.

White water rafting

The Las Cuevas river, fed by water from the Aconcagua area, becomes the River Mendoza after Punta de Vacas. As it descends into the valley there are centres for water sports, particularly rafting.

The three most prominent rafting companies are Argentina Rafting, Betacourt Rafting and Rios Andinos. Argentina Rafting has its main office in Mendoza on Peatonal Sarmiento 223, Tel 429 0029. They will take clients from Mendoza to their Potrerillos centre (near the Vallecitos turn-off). The company also offers trekking, horse trekking and rock climbing. Events are well organised and a weekly programme is set. The Potrerillos centre has a good café.

Vallecitos

There is only one hostel in Vallecitos, the Ski y Montañas, catering for 40 people. The bedrooms have bunk beds, with 4, 6, 8 or 10 per room. There are four bathrooms. The costs are low, but the standard is quite basic.

LOS PENITENTES AND PUENTE DEL INCA

The Ayelen in Los Penitentes is divided into a hotel and hosteria. Open 365 days a year, the Ayelen's Hosteria will charge under half for a bunk bed in a four person dormitory as the hotel of the same name next door. There is little to choose between the quality of the hotel and the hosteria. Dinner in the Ayelen can be relatively expensive, whereas a meal in the hosteria café is cheaper, quicker and less formal. The Ayelen hotel was given a limited facelift in 2003; its main advantage may be the central heating.

An alternative to the Ayelen is across the road in the Cruz de Caña. There are 70 beds here in 3, 4 and 5 person bedrooms, and in a large dormitory. The cost is less than the Ayelen Hosteria, and they will offer just bed and breakfast, or B+B with either dinner or lunch.

In Puente del Inca, the Hosteria Puente del Inca has the word Hospedaje over the entrance door. It has 92 beds in 3, 4, 5 and 6 person bedrooms, with a bathroom per room. The costs for bed and breakfast, and evening meal if desired, are very cheap.

Contact with the army hostel, Ejercito Argentina, will have to be in Spanish. The cost per night is very reasonable, including a fine breakfast.

Street scene at Puente del Inca

SANTIAGO

Electricity is at 220V/50Hz, with two-pronged round pin plugs. There are a number of tourist offices, one in the Plaza de Armas and another on Providencia.

Places to stay

For the visitor the two obvious choices of districts to stay in are Downtown (or Central) Santiago or Providencia. If you take the public bus from outside the terminal building at the airport it will drop you at the end of the line at Los Heroes Bus Terminal and Metro station. This is Downtown Santiago.

If you search the internet for hotels in Santiago there are hundreds, in all price ranges, all bookable on-line. The following may be of some help.

Along Santiago's main street, the Alameda – Av Bernardo O'Higgins

– there is the imposing structure of Iglesia San Francisco. This is between the metro stations of Universidad de Chile and Santa Lucia. Behind and beside the church there is a range of hotels. On Paseo Paris there are three hotels, Hotel Paris, Hotel Londres and Hotel Vegas.

Hotel Paris continues to be popular because it is in most guidebooks. However, it no longer has any internal courtyard/garden, is cramped and serves a poor breakfast in a tiny room. Best value of the three is Hotel Vegas, where the rooms are spacious and clean, the attention to guests is first class and the breakfast is enormous.

Although this is the centre of town, the streets behind Iglesia San Francisco are bustling during the day with students, but quiet and safe at night.

An alternative hotel location is Baquedano, at the junction of the Alameda and Vicuna Mackenna. This is a very convenient place to stay, and there are a number of hotels.

Hotel Principado de Asturias on Ramon Carnicer has a reasonable apart hotel and a better main hotel. The Principado hotel on Vicuna MacKenna is cheap, but needs refurbishment. All are very conveniently located beside the Baquedano metro. A short walk takes one into the Bellavista district, where there is a public park, a zoo, and a throbbing nightlife of restaurants and street markets.

Hotel Durato on Augustinas is closer to the main shopping areas and even less expensive.

In Providencia there are many hotels suitable for all pockets. At the junction of 11 de Septiembre and Pedro de Valdivia there is the Hotel Neruda. This has a main hotel and an aparthotel. In the laneway to the side there is an entrance leading to Hotel Cambiaso Aparthotel, a small aparthotel that occupies the upper floors of the building. Rooms are generous and cheap, but no breakfast is provided.

There is a reasonably priced hostel opposite Los Heroes bus station on Tucapel Jimeniz 24, called the Che Lagarto.

Eating out

There are plenty of café and bars in the city serving Western and Chilean food, including many McDonald's, for instance on Alameda beside the Universidad de Chile metro and on 11 de Septiembre in Providencia. These are open all week, some continuing

Street scene in Santiago

to serve into the early morning. All of the restaurants, however, close on Sundays and most are also closed on Saturday evening.

There are four restaurant areas in Santiago, Bellavista, El Bosque Norte, Santa Lucia and Providencia. The Bellavista district under San Cristobal is a walk up from the Baquedano metro station, on the edge of Downtown Santiago. Alternatively, a taxi ride to the corner of Constitucion and Dardignac will reveal a choice of restaurants in easy reach.

La Bohéme is a good quality French restaurant at Constitucion 124. Their crevettes boheme is a chilled prawn cocktail in a tomato sauce. Try the sauté d'agneau a la biére (lamb on the bone), and maybe finish with a trio of sorbets.

El Bosque Norte, near Tobalaba metro, has many Western style bars and restaurants, including an English pub, an Irish pub and a German beer garden. The cuisine is distinctly Western and so are the prices.

In Providencia, between the Alameda and the river, behind Los Leones metro, there are restaurants with a more Chilean flavour. The Providencia district is compact, and there are also Western style, Chinese and other restaurants in the area.

The Santa Lucia restaurant area is mainly centred on Merced and the streets south of it and between Cerro Santa Lucia and Parque Forestal. On Merced there is a small French restaurant, Les Assassins, on one side of the

144

street, and La Terraza de Cerro on the other side. The latter serves excellent fish dishes.

The Los Buenos Muchachos restaurants provide meals accompanied by entertainment. These rather large establishments serve the best steaks while putting on a floorshow of typical Chilean dance and culture. There is one in the suburbs and one nearer the city centre on Ricardo Cumming. They are reasonably priced, and therefore very popular, so a booking is advisable.

To experience a real piece of Chilean life one should go to Mercado Central for a fish lunch. Even if fish is not to your liking the experience is worthwhile. Bring a camera. The restaurants are open (and particularly busy) on Sundays when other restaurants are closed.

The enormous steel structure of Mercado Central is close to Cal y Canto metro, and can seat 800 customers. Around the restaurant are many bustling fish stalls. Dónde Augusto is the largest of the restaurants in the market, and serves huge portions, so eat the starter before ordering another course. The paila marina is a mixed seafood soup that might be more aptly described as a fish stew. Try the conger eel, and do not leave without tasting the postre of mote con huesillo (peach in syrup).

Acuario is a small, quiet restaurant on Paris 817 serving good food at a very reasonable cost.

Donde Augusto restaurant in Mercado Central Santiago

For those wanting to sample traditional Chilean cuisine, *pastel de chocho* and *cazuela de ave* are popular in the Santiago area. *Barros Luco* is a sandwich of thin slices of meat topped with melted cheese.

If time or energy is not available for wine excursions there are many excellent wine establishments in the city. Try The Wine House on El Bosque Norte, or Vinoteca Isidora on Goyenechan.

Gear shops

The ChileMontana shop and Andesgear are both in Providencia. In the El Bosque Norte district, on the corner of Helvecia and Ebro, there are two shops side-by-side, Patagonia Gear and another Andesgear.

La Cumbre will almost certainly have all that the mountaineer needs, and the best quality, but it is rather expensive. This German-owned shop is on Av Apoquindo 5258, approximately 1km beyond the metro station Esc Militar on the left. Doite is a Chilean brand of excellent quality camping and mountaineering gear, from clothes, to pots and pans, to tents. It is all made in Korea. LIPPI is a brand of Chilean-made clothes that is good and inexpensive. The products are widely available in the gear shops.

Hiring gear is not popular in Chile. Limited supplies, however, are available at Patagonia Sport in Providencia. Alternatively, The Federación de Andinismo de Chile, whose website is www.feach.cl, may be helpful.

Foreign embassies

- **Australian Embassy**
  Isidora Goyenechea 3621
  Pisos 12 y 13
  Las Condes
  Santiago de Chile
  Chile
  Tel: 550 3500
  Fax: 331 5960 (DFAT)
  Embassy: consular.santiago@
  dfat.gov.au
  Visas and Immigration:
  dima-santiago@dfat.gov.au
  Hours: Mon–Fri: 8.30am–4.55pm
  Hours for Visas and Immigration:
  9.00am–11.30am.
  Metro Station: Alcantara
  www.chile.embassy.gov.au

- **Canadian Embassy**
  Nueva Tajamar 481
  12th floor.
  Las Condes
  Tel: (56 2) 652 3800
  Fax: (56 2) 652 3912
  Hours: Mon–Thu: 8.30am–5.30pm;
  Fri: 8.30am–1.00pm
  Metro Station: Tobalaba
  www.dfait-maeci.gc.ca/santiago
  stago@international.gc.ca

- **Embassy of New Zealand**
  Avenida El Golf 99, Of. 703
  Las Condes
  Tel: (56 2) 290 9802
  Fax: (56 2) 207 2333
  Hours: Mon–Thu: 9.00am–1.00pm,
  2.00pm–6.00pm; Fri:
  9.00am–1.30pm
  Metro Station: Alcantara
  embajada@nzembassy.cl

OTHER EMBASSIES IN SANTIAGO	
Austria ☎ 223 4774	**Italy** ☎ 470 8400
Czech Republic ☎ 231 1910	**Norway** ☎ 234 2888
France ☎ 225 1030	**Spain** ☎ 235 2755
Germany ☎ 463 2500	**Sweden** ☎ 231 2733
Holland ☎ 223 6825	**Switzerland** ☎ 263 4211

- **South African Embassy**
  Avenida 11 de Septiembre 2353
  16th floor, Torre San Ramón
  Providencia
  Tel: (56 2) 231 2860
  Fax: (56 2) 231 3185
  Hours: Mon–Thu: 9.00am–4.30pm;
  Fri: 9.00am–1.00pm
  Metro Station: Los Leones
  www.embajada-sudafrica.cl
  info@embajada-sudafrica.cl

- **UK Embassy**
  Avenida El Bosque Norte 0125
  Las Condes
  Tel: (56 2) 370 4100
  Fax: (56 2) 335 5988
  Hours: Mon–Thu: 9.00am–1.00pm;
  2.00pm–5.30pm
  Metro Station: Apoquindo
  www.britemb.cl
  embsan@britemb.cl

Sunset over Berlin Camp

- **US Embassy**
  Andrés Bello 2800
  Las Condes
  Tel: (56 2) 232 2600
  Fax: (56 2) 330 3710
  Hours: Mon–Fri: 8.30am–5.00pm
  Metro Station: Apoquindo
  www.usembassy.cl

TUPUNGATO

The website www.peakware.com is a source of information on Tupungato. It is a receptacle for personal experiences on the mountain. Those listed as providing services on Aconcagua are generally available to provide similar services on Tupungato. Chile Montana and Aventuras Patagonicas have guided treks throughout the summer.

There are two hotels in Tupungato, both on the main street, the Hotel Italia and the Hotel Turismo. The latter has the tourist office in the reception.

There are also two hosterias, the Don Romulo and the Refuge of the Condor.

APPENDIX 4
South American cuisine

Not Spanish...

A *bocadillo* may be a sandwich in Spain, but in South America it is a mixed food ball, generally vegetable. Sandwich is the common term here. A *bocadillo de acelga* is a ball mixture of chopped vegetables, cheese and garlic. A *bocadito* is a small item of food, generally a piece of chocolate taken with coffee.

There are no *tapas* (snacks at a bar or before a meal), but you may be served *picadas*, the regional equivalent.

Mantequilla is butter in Spain and in Chile, but *manteca* is the more common name in Argentina.

Snacks and starter courses

A common picada in a restaurant or café is simply *pan amasado* and *pebre*. Pan amasado is home-made bread, generally pitta bread, and pebre is a sauce of hot chilli peppers, tomatoes and garlic in olive oil. This will often be placed on the table as an appetiser before a meal. *Matambre arollado* is a paté of vegetables and meat.

By far the most popular snack in South America is an *empanada*. This is similar to an English Cornish pasty – minced meat and chopped potato inside pastry. Variations include some chopped vegetables in the mix. However, the empanada has expanded into cheese (*queso*) and

even sweet varieties. They are always hot, made and sold on the side of the road out of insulated carriers at the border, or presented as starters at even the smartest of restaurants. Even McDonald's serves empanadas in Santiago.

Tortas are semi-sweet bread rolls. *Alfajores* are sweet cake sandwiches, usually with chocolate inside. *Kurchen* is a pie.

Many sweet cakes and biscuits are made with *dulce de leche*. This mixture of glucose, maize, sugar and milk, is a near obsession in Argentina and is applied like jam or peanut butter to many foodstuffs – apples, biscuits, and even cheese.

Meat dishes

Fish will often be on the menu in Santiago, but virtually never in Mendoza. Here beef is king. *Bife*, pure beef, comes in many cuts and preparations. *Bife de Chorizo* is the prime form, simply grilled sirloin, or chateaubriand. Bife de Chorizo is a common term in Argentina, but not quite so universal, except in Santiago, in Chile. How long it is to be grilled for is easy – one quarter (*uno quarto*), half (*medio*), tres quartos or *punto*.

Carne is meat. *Asado* is barbecued meat. *Estofado* is a stew. A

Empanadas and pan amasadó being cooked at a roadside café

popular meal in Argentina is *porilla* or *porillada*, which is a portion of three different meats – beef/steak, black pudding (*morcilla*) and sausage (*chorizo*)– all grilled. Additional servings of the beef/steak are generally provided at no extra cost.

A *lomito* is a steak sandwich, traditionally in pitta bread, garnished with slices of salad, mayonnaise and tomato sauce. In the cities the pitta bread may be replaced with French bread. A *lomito completo* has a fried egg added to the sandwich. A *chacarero* sandwich is very similar to a lomito, but the meat comes in thin, lean strips. A *barros luco* is a sandwich with thin strips of steak and hot cheese.

Arollado chancho is rolled pork. *Riñon al Jerez* is kidneys in sherry sauce.

Fish dishes

Sopa surtido de mariscos is a shellfish soup. Fresh fish of trout (*trucha*), hake (*merluza*), sea trout (*corvine*) and salmon (*salmon*) are common in Chilean restaurants. Some specialist restaurants will also have unusual varieties on the menu, such as flounder (*lenguado*), tuna (*atun*), conger eel (*congria*) and shellfish (*mariscos*).

Desserts

Postre is the Spanish for dessert. The most common postres are flans, jellies (*gelatine*) and ice-cream (*helado*).

Higos en almíbar is figs in syrup, and *alcayota con nuez* is a syrup of string fruit with nuts.

Drinks

Wine is cheap and plentiful in both countries. Between them Argentina and Chile produce wine using the same range of grape varieties as Europe or North America. They also have their own particular grapes – notably Carmenére in Chile and Malbec in Argentina.

The weather is not as temperamental here as in France or other countries, and all vineyards are irrigated, so that particular vintages are not so important. The South Americans virtually always oak their wines, generally in French and American oak barrels (some are currently trying the much cheaper Chinese barrels), but the degree of oak ageing is not as high as in Australia or, indeed, Spain.

The Carmanére vine was brought from France in the 18th century, where it was as popular in Bordeaux as cabernet sauvignon. After the phylloxera the vine was never returned to France, because the French had never been able to achieve good yields from it. Effectively the Carmanére grape died out. Then in the 1990s during DNA testing of Chilean merlot grapes it was rediscovered, and in the space of a few years Carmanére rose from obscurity to become the national grape of Chile. At a wine fair in Santiago in 2003, every wine producer had samples of Carmanére for tasting. *Pais* is a simple, local wine.

Beer (*cerveza*) in South America nearly always comes in half-litre or one-litre bottles. Very similar to Western lager, the brand names of Andes, Quilmes and Brahma are popular in Argentina, while Castel and Estudo are similar brands in Chile. The alcohol
150

content is low at under five per cent, so mountaineers need have little fear.

In the Potrerillos area the brand name Jerome is available. This beer comes in three flavours – *negra* (black), *roja* (red) and *rubia* (blonde). The rubia is very similar to a lager. The roja could be likened to an English light ale, whilst the negra has a slightly bitter taste.

Pisco Sour is a most popular aperitif or cocktail, particularly in Chile. It is a mixture of pisco wine, egg white, lemon juice and sugar. Pisco wine is made in Chile from muscatel grapes and can be purchased in a number of different concentrations.

Chicha is a grape cider, very harsh and high in alcohol content, usually only available in the countryside. In the north chicha is a milky beer, made from maize.

Fish dishes at Mercado Central

APPENDIX 5
Spanish–English language notes

Language necessity

Few ordinary Argentineans speak English, and even fewer Chileans. Those who interface directly with climbers, such as guides, will have a reasonable command of English, but the arrieros, the doctor, the airline official and the bus conductor are unlikely to have any.

On the mountain, salutations in Spanish are the norm. For those making an unguided expedition, a reasonable command of Spanish is recommended, if not essential. Even for those who have hired guides there will be many occasions when a basic knowledge of Spanish is desirable.

South American Spanish

South American Spanish has some dissimilarities with European Spanish, for instance, how to pronounce words including the letter 'c'. In South America the language is softer, less harsh than in Spain. Argentinean Spanish is different from Chilean Spanish, but the Spanish of Mendoza is more like Chilean. Chileans speak very fast. They regularly drop the 's' from the middle and ends of words, and they use many slang words and words with their origin in the native Indian. *Buenos dias* will be heard as *Bueno dia*, and *Como estas* as *Como eta*.

Addressing people

In Spain and all Latin American countries there is the formal *usted* and the informal *tu*. In Argentina they also use a third form of address, *vos*. Let's look at an example: a guide I met addressed his father formally with *usted*, whereas the father reciprocated with the informal *tu*. When the guide spoke to the arrieros he used the intermediate *vos*, but when they addressed him it was formally using *usted*. He spoke to me formally, even though I persisted in speaking informally to him.

In Chile the formalities are not so strict, and vos is not used.

The basics

The basics of Spanish, however, hold. These will be found in phrasebooks and dictionaries. They include:
- h is always silent
- j is pronounced similar to 'ch' in Scottish loch
- ll is pronounced like 'y' in loyal
- n is pronounced like 'ni' in onion
- v is pronounced like a 'b'. However, in many parts of South America the pronunciation is as a 'v'.

Listed below are some of the names and common words or expressions that may be encountered, pronounced in the Mendoza-Chile style, with their English equivalent.

Proper nouns

Words ending in *agua* such as Aconcagua and Rancagua are pronounced aawaa. There are a few differing interpretations of the origin of Aconcagua. Some postulate that it is derived from the Quecha Language:

- Akun = Summit
- Ka = Other
- Agua = Fearful

Others suggest it is Aymara and translates to Sentinel of Stone.

Argentina	The 'g' is pronounced as in get
Quebrada	Deep stream
Casa del Cura	House of the priest
Casa de Piedra	House of stone
Cerro Mirador	Mountain viewpoint
Cristo Redentor	Christ the Redeemer
Chile	Pronounced a softer 'chiily'
Las Cuevas	The caves
Cordón del Plata	The string or line of the silver
Cresta del Viento	Windy crest
Ejercito	Army
Estancia	Ranch or farm
La Hoyada	The pit, pothole
Mendoza	Pronounce the 'z' as in English
Lomas Blancas	White hills
La Olla	The cooking pot
Pabellón	Pavilion, tent
Penitentes	Standing icicles
Plata	Silver
Plomo	Lead (metal)
Portezuelo de Fraile	Col of the friar
Punta de Vacas	The point of (the river of) cows
Puente del Inca	Bridge of the Incas
Pampas Leñas	Plain where there is firewood
Rocas Blancas	White rocks
El Salto	The jump or leap
Valle de Las Vacas	Valley of the cows
Vallecitos	Little valleys (*Buy-ay-see-tos*)

Salutations

Hola	Hello
Buenos días	Good day/good morning
Buenas tardes	Good afternoon
Buenas noches	Good evening/night
Adíos	Goodbye
Hasta luego	See you later
Cómo estás	How are you?
Muy bien, y tú	Very good, and you?
Buen provecho	Bon appétit

Numbers

0	*Cero*
1	*Uno*
2	*Dos*
3	*Tres*
4	*Cuatro*
5	*Cinco*
6	*Seis*
7	*Siete*
8	*Ocho*
9	*Nueve*
10	*Diez*
11	*Once*
12	*Doce*
13	*Trece*
14	*Catorce*
15	*Quince*
16	*Dieciséis*
17	*Diecisiete*
18	*Dieciocho*
19	*Diecinueve*
20	*Veinte*
21	*Veintiuno*
29	*Veintinueve*
30	*Treinta*
32	*Treinta y dos*
40	*Cuarenta*
50	*Cincuenta*
60	*Sesanta*
70	*Setenta*
80	*Ochenta*
90	*Noventa*
100	*Cien*
110	*Ciento diez*
500	*Quinientos*
1000	*Mil*
2000	*Dos Mil*
Million	*Un millón*

The alphabet

A	a	Aconcagua
B	be	Bilbao
C	ce	Carmen
Ch	che	Champiñon
D	de	Deportivo
E	e	Español
F	efe	Francia
G	khe	Go
H	aache	Hasta
I	ee	Isabel
J	khota	José
K	ka	Kilo
L	ele	Londres
Ll	elye	Tortilla
M	eme	Metro
N	ene	Noches
O	o	Otro
P	pe	Puente
Q	koo	Quisiera
R	ere	Río
S	ese	Sábado
T	te	Tardes
U	oo	Uno
V	oobay	Viento
W	oobay doblay	Washington
X	ekees	Taxi
Y	eegriayge	Paraguay
Z	theta	Zeta

Days

Monday	Lunes
Tuesday	Martes
Wednesday	Miércoles
Thursday	Jueves
Friday	Viernes
Saturday	Sábado
Sunday	Domingo

Months

January	Enero
February	Febrero
March	Marzo
April	Abril
May	Mayo
June	Junio
July	Julio
August	Agosto
September	Septiembre
October	Octubre
November	Noviembre
December	Diciembre

Seasons

Spring	La Primavera
Summer	El Verano
Autumn	El Otoño
Winter	El Invierno

Colours

Black	negro
Blue	azul
Brown	marrón
Cream	crema
Gold	dorado
Green	verde
Grey	gris
Orange	naranja
Red	rojo
Silver	plateado
White	blanco
Yellow	amarillo

Shapes

Big	grande
Fat	gordo/a
Flat	llano/a
Long	largo/a
Narrow	estrecho/a
Round	redondo/a
Small	pequeño/a
Tall	alto/a
Thin	delgado
Tiny	pequeñito

Food

Apple	manzana (manthana)
Banana	la plátano
Biscuits	las galletas
Bread	el pan
Bread roll	el panecillo
Butter	la mantequilla (manteca in Argentina)
Cheese	el queso
Chicken	el pollo
Chips	las papas fritas
Eggs	los huevos
Garlic	la ajo
Ham	el jamón

153

Honey	la miel
Jam	la marmelada
Marmalade	la marmelada de naranja
Milk	la leche
Mushrooms	los champiñones
Mustard	la mostaza
Onion	la cebolla
Pepper	la pimienta
Potatoes	las papas
Prawns	las gambas
Rice	el arroz
Salt	la sal
Steak	el bistec or bife
Stew	el estofado

A portion of..	una ración de…
Breakfast	el desayuno
Lunch	la comida, el almuerzo
Dinner	la cena
Plate	el plato
Boiled	hervido
Fried	frito
Grilled	a la parrilla
Roast	asado
Scrambled	revueltos
Stewed	cocido, guisado
Rare	poco hecho, or uno quarto
Medium	normal, or medio
Well done	bien hecho, or a punto
Menu	la carta
Set menu	el menu del día

Dedos	Fingers
Dedo del pie	Toe
Despacio	Slowly
Dolor de cabeza	Headache
Este	East
Excusado	Toilet
Gafas de sol	Sunglasses
Helada	Frost
Linterna	Torch
Lugar de campamento	Campsite
Neblina	Mist
Nieve	Snow
Norte	North
Nube	Cloud
Oeste	West
Peligro	Danger
Pie	Foot
Precipicio	Cliff
Rappel	Rock climbing
Refugio	Shelter
Resbaladizo	Slippery
Saco de dormir	Sleeping bag
Sur	South
Siga derecho	Keep straight ahead
Tienda de deportes	Sports shop

Spanish words you might need to recognise for mountaineering

Acarreo	Loose stones, scree
Aceite bronceador	Suntan oil
Altura	Altitude, height
Ampolla	Blister
Aseos	Toilets
Botella	Bottle
Brújula	Compass
Cabalgata	Trekking on horseback
Caminata	Trek
Camping	Campsite
Casco	Helmet
Cerro	Mountain
Cima, cumbre	Summit
Colchón neumático	Air bed
Congelado	Frozen
Cordillera	Mountain range

NOTES

LISTING OF CICERONE GUIDES

For full and up-to-date information
on our ever-expanding list of guides,
please visit our website:
www.cicerone.co.uk.

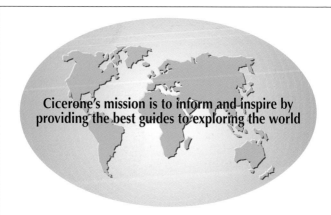

Cicerone's mission is to inform and inspire by providing the best guides to exploring the world

Since its foundation 40 years ago, Cicerone has specialised in publishing guidebooks and has built a reputation for quality and reliability. It now publishes nearly 300 guides to the major destinations for outdoor enthusiasts, including Europe, UK and the rest of the world.

Written by leading and committed specialists, Cicerone guides are recognised as the most authoritative. They are full of information, maps and illustrations so that the user can plan and complete a successful and safe trip or expedition – be it a long face climb, a walk over Lakeland fells, an alpine cycling tour, a Himalayan trek or a ramble in the countryside.

With a thorough introduction to assist planning, clear diagrams, maps and colour photographs to illustrate the terrain and route, and accurate and detailed text, Cicerone guides are designed for ease of use and access to the information.

If the facts on the ground change, or there is any aspect of a guide that you think we can improve, we are always delighted to hear from you.

Cicerone Press
2 Police Square Milnthorpe Cumbria LA7 7PY
Tel: 015395 62069 Fax: 015395 63417
info@cicerone.co.uk www.cicerone.co.uk

CICERONE